The

Naked Truth

About

Hedonism II

A naughty but nice guide to Jamaica's all-inclusive, very adult resort

Chris Santilli

ISBN: 0-9662683-1-8
Library of Congress Catalog Card Number: 97-91394

First printing: April 1998
Second printing: October 1998

Book cover design: No. 9 Design, Inc., Chicago

Scarlett, Oh! Publishing makes this book available at special discounts for bulk purchases. For information, call or write:

Scarlett, Oh! Publishing
P.O. Box 6584
Villa Park, Ill. 60181-6584
888-883-9040 (book order fulfillment)
E-mail: Books@wordcrafting.com
http://www.wordcrafting.com

Scarlett, Oh! Publishing is a fun division of Wordcrafting, Villa Park, Ill.
Printed in the United States of America.

Dedication

Many wonderful people contributed their thoughts, quotes, and pictures to this book. Because of the privacy I promised, I cannot name them all.

Know that any guest of Hedonism II who is identifiable in this book has provided me with written permission to use his or her image or name. Respect for privacy is a huge concern of the hotel's guests. And *respect* is the key to making the Hedo experience the most fun.

Doug Bowen contributed more than his fair share of wit to these pages. For that and his love and support, I thank him the most.

Doug's alternative titles for this book:

Perverts of the Caribbean
Everything I Know About Life I Learned at Hedonism II
An Adult Summer Camp Guidebook
You're Not in Kansas Anymore
PJs, DJs, and BJs

Contents

Chapter 5: Entertainment in this land beyond Kansas 123

BARNES & NOBLE
STORE 2587 CEDAR RAPIDS, IA 319-393-4800

REG#04   BOOKSELLER#030
RECEIPT#   6698 04/18/99   11:15 AM

S 0966268318   NAKED TRUTH ABT HEDONISM
                1 @ 19.95   19.95

SUBTOTAL   19.95
SALES TAX - 5%   1.00
TOTAL   20.95
CHECK PAYMENT   20.95

VISIT US ONLINE!

BARNESANDNOBLE.COM
AOL KEYWORD: BN

Introduction

Travel brochures tell you Hedonism II is set on 22 acres at the northern end of Negril's seven-mile beach, about 55 miles west of Montego Bay in Jamaica. One prepaid price pays for all meals, room, entertainment, and booze at the resort. The brochure pictures youthful women and men bouncing around.

This book tells you what the travel brochures won't— what to really expect at Hedonism II. This book is *not* sponsored by Hedonism II or its owner, SuperClubs.

Hedonism II, often called Hedo, is like no other hotel in the world, which accounts for its huge repeat clientele. At any given time, almost one-third of its guests are repeaters and another third came on the direct recommendation of a Hedo veteran.

Guests of Hedo experiment with whatever they consider exotic: be it swinging on the trapeze, floating naked on a raft, or dancing on the stage in a bed sheet in front of 500 people.

Some guests can't tell friends and family they go to Hedo because of the resort allows some nudity. And many travel agents don't recommend Hedo because of its sordid reputation. The hotel's general manager Kevin Levee says Hedo's reputation is unfair.

The myths are unfair, but truth is truth. Stories abound at Hedo, and I've collected some here. The place *is* unreal at times. But Hedo is mostly like the real world: filled with all types of people. Although I describe some extreme examples, Hedo is a normal beach vacation for most.

I go to Hedo because the friends made there are the best. Oh, and the maintenance is low—the wonderful staff feeds me, entertains me, watches over me, and cleans up after me.

Irie,

Chris Santilli

Chapter 1

Be wrecked for a week

Hedonism II is synonymous with the word *panties*. Panties conjure an image of naughty but nice. Panties are what you make of them. So is Hedo.

Where else can three chubby gray-haired guys dance on stage in women's panties, sing a parody honoring Marv Albert, and receive loud kudos? (Thanks, Carlotta, Benita, and Barrita.)

Hedo (hee'doe) is also like the Internet, where you survive on your cleverness, wit, articulation, and charm—not your bank roll, good looks, and reputation.

> "Hedo is a keg party with class. You hold your beer cup with your pinkie extended."
>
> —Doug from Pennsylvania

Hedo is about attitude, freedom, and giggles. Sex and booze only highlight the experience; they are not the main event. Hedo is an adult kid camp where friends meet time and again.

Sit in the dining area at 1:30 a.m. The scene is near most as bustling as it is at lunch. This place never sleeps. And no kids are running around. Guests must be 18 or older.

Hedo has been called Heavenism, Club Hedo, Camp Hedo, and Hedolicious. The Jamaicans call it "The Zoo."

"I first went to Hedonism II in 1983 and had no idea what to expect. My husband did not even tell me the name of the place we were going to until we were on Air Jamaica and well in the air. He had only told me we were going to an all-inclusive resort in Jamaica that offered scuba diving.

When he told me about the place and showed me the brochure, I hit the ceiling. I thought we would not even be able to walk on the beach without stepping on copulating couples. We had a huge fight all the way to the resort, and I assured him that he had ruined our vacation.

In November 1997, we returned for our 20th visit to our favorite place. We have made many friends over the years, many of whom return at the same time each year as we do. Hedo is about fun, laughter, friendship, and a bit about loosening your inhibitions."

—Jennifer from Atlanta

What you see at Hedo might not be what you think it is. That girl in an itsy-bitsy dress who is dry-humping the leg of a gray-haired man at the main bar is *not* sleeping with him, or anyone else. Those women dancing erotically together are *not* lesbians. And that man with the inflatable sheep—he's only a *little* perverted.

Tales from the Naked City

Walking home one night I found a big white pair of Hanes Her Way underpants on the sidewalk. I hung them on the doorknob of the room with the sign that read: "Sacrifices now in progress and we're running low on virgins."

Hedo inspires enormous loyalty among those who go. You meet wonderful people who make leaving difficult. Back at home people suffer from Dreaded Island Fever, which makes them come back to Hedo again and again. A sure sign of DIF is logging onto Frank and Marcey's web site to listen to the tree frogs recorded there to get to sleep on your first night back *(see Chapter 6, Use the Internet for Year-Round Hedo)*.

As surreal as Hedo can seem, it's just like the real world—only without the maintenance and without the criticism for being silly or naughty.

Tales from the Naked City

Two women were able to paint all 10 toes on a sober guy standing at the nude beach bar without him knowing it. A slow process, but full of glorious moments. When he realized it and laughed...to much applause...he merely asked how long he had to stay out of the sand. He later asked for polish remover, but the women told him they only had fingernail polish remover, and the island was out of toenail polish remover so he was out of luck.

You find nicer accommodations and better food at many hotels around the world. The Caribbean sports hundreds—maybe thousands—of places where the water pressure is more reliable. Hedo manager Kevin Levee says he has "a mandate to fix the water problem." The repeat guests all snicker to themselves.

But water pressure and luxury aren't what Hedo is all about. And Hedo is not about swingers and sex in the hot tub late at night either—even though everyone seems to want to pray to St. Mattress of the Springs.

"Hedo is about sun, sand, sea, sex, sunsets, and the last day: sunrise."

—Gail and Pee Wee

These buttoxen (plural of buttocks) represent the myth of Hedonism II. Although these ladies are guests of the resort, they are the exception rather than the rule.

A woman who stays on the prude beach under the trees says Hedo is about relaxing and not being pressured into activities à la Club Med, a Lifestyler says Hedo is about the sex parties, and a nudist says it's about the pleasant social atmosphere. And they are all right.

Sometimes it's wild; sometimes it's mild. But everyone cuts loose from the norm.

A married man says he couldn't pry the smile off his face after his first Hedo experience: "We hadn't stepped foot in the hotel more than 10 minutes, when the staff got me involved in the 'Best Bodies in Motion' contest. The next thing I know I'm dancing naked in front of 16 beautiful girls who are pouring beer all over me and licking it off. And the trip only got better after that."

4

Hedo isn't for everyone, though. Not everyone appreciates the public noodle frontity or the sensual atmosphere where inhibitions often melt away.

"Hedo management and guests fortunately do not impose on others the public behavior standards of the average U.S. citizen. (*USA Today* reported that 43% of us are now reborn Christians.) Other resorts cater to wholesomeness because they are concerned about losing money. Most people are uptight about any kind of sexual expression in public. Rather than walk away from scenes they do not enjoy, many of the righteous types would rather complain that they are unable to maintain their uptight lifestyle in every square inch of the resort. The folks who are afraid they somehow might lose their virtue should go elsewhere and not try to discourage Hedo from offering a real alternative."

—Bill Schwemer from Virginia, married, age 57

"Hedonism II has evolved over the years. It is guest driven," says general manager Kevin Levee. "We just let friendships form. It's not your standard family vacation."

No kidding. But he's right. People make Hedo what it is, regardless of the changes that might occur there. And an important part of those people are the staff of the hotel.

At Hedo, a repeat guest might be wrapped in a welcome home sweaty bear hug from Tony at the entrance. Paulette greets you at the front desk with a huge smile. Faye in reservations always beams when she sees a familiar face and makes sure everything is going smoothly for you.

As you make your way through the dining area, Teddy cocks his head to the side and shakes your hand warmly telling you "Respect." Cleopatra teasingly clears her throat behind you to get your attention before she asks if you would like coffee, and then she tells you how good it is to see you again.

On the nude beach, Delroy calls out your name as you approach the bar, and Scumba performs the ritual respect handshake. Jazzbo makes sure you don't lose your shoes in the sand—and you know his grin extends to his eyes, even though you'll never see them behind his dark glasses.

Repeat guests all want to be considered Jamericans, but Veronica, the patron saint and eponymous bartender of the piano bar, is the only true Jamerican. (Remember to get her on your team for the erstwhile "Name That Tune" competition.)

These people, and so many others, are the staff of Hedo. Their incredible dedication to their work and their many kindnesses cannot be overstated. They make Hedo pleasant and comfortable. And their friendship grows with each trip.

> "We're going back to Hedo to wade through the gunk in the tub; laugh at the drunk, amorous single guys; struggle with tying a toga; listen to the crappy music in the disco; just say no to ganja; get my buns sunburned; search in vain for towels; stand in line for drinks; have no water pressure; get sand everywhere; see the same shows as last time; have a wild bus ride; wonder why it costs so much money; be kept awake by tree frogs; wonder when the weird things in the hot tub happen; eat mediocre food; screw around with that dangly thing they give you to keep your room key on; and bitch and moan about everything I can think of.
>
> And all the while, having a really great vacation, enjoying every minute of not being at work, and never being able to get that goofy grin off my face. Hey, what can I say? I'm a sucker for a place I love."
>
> —Greg from Oklahoma City

This is one of the naked truths about Hedonism II: Tranquility on a raft.

Frequently asked questions

Most questions about Hedo have to do with naked nudity, sex, who goes there, and what to wear. Here are the basics.

Nakedness

Is Hedo a nudist place?

No, Hedo is not a nudist resort. Guests are not naked all the time. Some people do experience déjà nude and forget to put on clothes. Nudity is only allowed within the walking area of the nude-side rooms and at the nude beach and nude pool complex. That's well under a third of the total Hedo campus. Topless is permitted but not overly common on the prude beach and at the prude swimming pool and hot tub.

On Thursday's Toga night, nudity is allowed at dinner. On Tuesday's Pyjama night, nudity is allowed in the disco well after dinner. The secret rule is that nudity is allowed anywhere at Hedo after midnight, but the truth of that rule varies. Other than that, no nudity is allowed.

I'm nervous about the nude beach. What's it like?

Fun. Get over it. Life's too short. Get naked. The second hardest thing about the nude beach at Hedo is taking your clothes off the first time. The hardest thing is putting them back on. *(See Chapter 3, Nudity Concerns Pass Quickly.)*

Butt writing (here, a birthday greeting) is a merry pastime for many Hedophiles.

Our previous experience with nudism is "no touchy-feelie" at resorts. That is, nude is not equated with sex.

Exactly and Hedo is different; it's *not* a nudist resort, but a lot of people are naked. Hedo has undertones of sexuality and oftentimes overtones too. Some weeks are sexier than others depending on who's there. Some times of the day (2 a.m. hot tub) are sexier than others. Hedo has touchy-feelie among friends who enjoy it. Occasionally someone will touch you in a way you think inappropriate, such as a fanny pat. Just let them know that doesn't fly with you with words or a stern look—just like in the real world.

Can I wear my bottoms on the nude beach?

Women, yes; Men, no. Attractive women wearing their bottoms will be looked at more than naked ones—as a curiosity and because clothes make most people look sexier. When some women have their period they wear bottoms—many just tuck the string up. Some weeks the "prude patrol" of guests is vociferous and may give you some fun-natured grief, but this is not frequent and they easily let up if you are pleasant.

My husband is concerned about getting aroused on the beach and not being able to hide it. Is this pretty common, and what advice can you give him to calm his anxiety about going to a nude beach for the first time?

"Wood on the beach!" is my favorite cry. Yup, wood happens, but it's rare. Just being naked is not overly sexual for most people. Some are proud of their wood and show it off (also rare). One young buck with wood said, "I can't help it." So some ladies put body stickers all over the wood for decoration and then ignored it.

For those who do find the nude beach titillating and want to squelch or hide their organ, use one of these techniques:

- Go into the water. All penises float so an erection just looks like a big floater.

- Lay face down on the beach chair. Do not make a humping motion without someone under you. (One man stuck it through the slats in the lounge at the edge of the shore, and the waves swept it forward and back as he slept.)

- Have someone laugh at you. Most will oblige.

- Put it to use on a raft or other place away from the crowd (with a woman, not by yourself), preferably not too hidden so we can watch, though. If you are really good, the guests applaud and cheer.

Masturbation on the nude beach is not socially acceptable and seldom seen outdoors.

How to dress

What do people wear at Hedo?

Everyone has a tropical summer wear look found at any Caribbean resort. At breakfast and lunch in the dining area, men and women dress in shorts and T-shirts, swimsuits (any type from big one-pieces with major support to minuscule thongs), and cover-ups or pareos.

Naked male chests are common at breakfast and lunch but not at dinner. Naked female chests are not allowed off the beach except for Toga (during dinner) or Pyjama nights (after dinner). At meals, women need only cover crotch and nipples, even with a sheer or loosely knit material.

At dinner, people dress nicer, though shorts and T-shirts are still plentiful. Skirts approximating belts are not uncommon. Men in kilts happen. Some wear long pants.

No one wears a jacket unless making a statement or being a dweeb... and the difference is in the seriousness with which the

the person is wearing it. One guy likes to wear a dinner jacket with no pants, so when he lifts his arms—whoops, there it is.

Sandals are always okay, but socks are ridiculous—this is the Tropics. It's hot almost all the time. Shoes are only required in the Pastafari restaurant. Shoes are wise, however, because glass breaks nightly.

Some women shop Sluts 'R Us and enjoy traipsing around in their spandex outfits and heels. Some people wear no underwear or shoes for the entire vacation—simply because they can. One friend just wraps a hotel bath towel around his hips and wears it everywhere, including Toga and PJ night. He packs light.

What do I need for the Toga party?

Hedo supplies the white, twin-size sheet. After cleaning your room on Thursday, the maid puts an extra sheet folded on top of your bed. Bring accessories, if you want, such as a belt, safety pins, gaudy jewelry, or headpieces. Do not wear underwear because the danger of having them removed by someone runs high.

How wild do people get on Pyjama and Toga nights?

Wild? As in clothes: Very. For PJ night: from naked to collars to severe bondage stuff to cutesy-wootsy to boxer shorts to full flannels with slippers and stuffed animal. Toga night can be judged by the number of breasts on display. A good Toga night shows at least nine breasts (some women wear a one-hooter-halter).

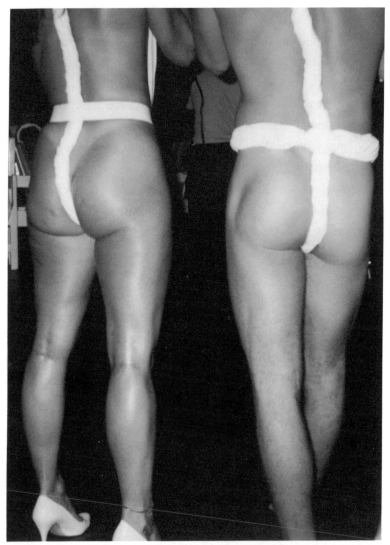

Some guests tie bed-sheet togas in revealing ways, but most opt for greater coverage.

Sex

Will the swingers try to make me have sex with them?

"Contrary to popular belief, people in 'the lifestyle' will not chase you down and make you have sex with them," says Vicki from Vegas. "You have to be somewhat aggressive if you want to have sex outside your marriage. No one spends time pursuing people who have no interest in swinging because too many other people are willing and want to play."

In the swinger lifestyle, the rules state: "No" always means "no, thank you." Swingers generally are notoriously fun and social people and will not lure you in or make you uncomfortable if you tell them "no." You can say, "Thanks for asking, but no thanks," with pleasant results. Were you to have a problem, use English to resolve it. Most people at Hedo speak English.

We're not into the lifestyle scene but don't want to alienate people by saying no all the time. How does that work?

Only people who want to exchange bodily fluids (and not socialize) will snub you. They are people into the total scores encountered, not the quality. They are the minority and you'll have a great time talking about their advances alone in your room later.

Do people really have sex in the hot tub or is that part of the Hedo hype?

Yes, sex in the hot tub occurs...as long as the guards aren't stopping it. The single men do stare, but they usually don't bother you. Sometimes lurkers aren't even there. I wouldn't worry about them. You can always leave and take your party elsewhere. You'll likely have no problems with sex on the beach at night—and with the chair cushions, pleasant beds can be made. Bring your bedspread to make your love nest cozier. At Hedo you can do a lot of things you wouldn't and can't do anywhere else.

Is there a lot of sex going on openly?

The vast majority of guests are *not* getting it on in public. Usually any open sex occurs among the same people. Many people go home disappointed because they never saw any open sex. Or, if you are like my friend Henry, sex goes on whenever you aren't around and stops whenever you appear, so you keep missing it. Hedo is not an orgy...but then again...sometimes that hot tub at 2 a.m. does become interesting.

The amount of open sex depends on the time of day or week. Hedo is a physical place (affection included) for some people, but you only go where you are invited, just like the real world.

People do giggle at one another's tits. They cup balls and give massages, but it's among friends—and you know who you can do this with if you have good socialization skills. And all of it is for fun, doesn't last too long, is usually done in a joking way, and doesn't result in orgasm.

How intrusive are the young single guys? Will they be hitting on my wife all the time?

Don't worry about it. Your wife can use English to thwart advances easily—but don't be disappointed if they don't occur. Seldom are advances uncomfortable or awkward. Yes, the rare occasion does occur that gets ugly, like in any part of the world, including your hometown, but never make it an issue in deciding whether to go to Hedo. Strong language should work for the rare person with severe rectal-cranial inversion. They'll always stare, though, because they can't help themselves. You may as well not leave your house if it's a big concern. The odds of it happening in the real world are as great as at Hedo.

Will I get laid?

Depends on if someone says yes to your advances—just like the real world. If you go to Hedo without a date and you are male, don't go to Hedo for the sex. Odds are you'll be disappointed. Women, however, enjoy the high ratio of men to women. *(See Chapter 4, Finding Partners at Hedo.)*

Who goes to Hedo?

Is everyone supermodel thin, or is there a range?

The range of people you see at home is the same range you'll see at Hedo. From hard bodies to what most of us are: lumpy. The Hedo brochures lie. But get over yourself—whether you are an Adonis or a chubbo.

Do repeater groups take over Hedo?

Repeater groups no longer make Hedo virgins uncomfortable—likely because they're getting quieter. Repeater groups tend to be couples and older. The last three weeks of January are especially heavy with Lifestylers. You find fewer singles at that time, but there are always singles there. Repeater groups can fill up to 60% of the resort, especially over Anniversary (Nov. 1) and many U.S. holidays. *(See Chapter 3, Repeaters Are Surprisingly Organized.)*

What's the type of person who goes to Hedo?

All types go there. The repeaters tend to be a little more affluent than the one-shot wonders out for their first, last, and only vacation of their lives. Some of the upscale ones wear the jewelry on the beach to show it; most do not. Every occupation goes there, from doctors and lawyers, to musicians and artists, to secretaries and truck drivers, to moms and retirees.

The guests are predominately white with 10% or so of other races. Generally, half are couples. Most guests are from the United States, but a large Canadian contingent is always there. Europeans and South Americans are gaining in numbers. The men tend to outnumber the women by 2 to 1, but some weeks seem 8 to 1.

The attitude, not the look, age, or money, of the person, makes a difference on whether fun is had at Hedo.

Tips for making a trip more fun

Beware the genital gnats. Seems that when talking to a bunch of friends while standing on the nude beach, someone always attracts the flying nonbiting bugs, much to everyone else's amusement. The only way to get rid of them is by drowning them in the pool or ocean.

Wear panties in the airplanes because the seats are hell on your bare butt.

Ignore whatever offends you, because you will see it all, especially if you're up late enough.

If you have to score, bring someone with you.

If you want to meet interesting people, belly up to the bar and strike up a conversation. You'll meet the friendliest people in the world at Hedo and some of the worst jerks. If no one is talking to you during your trip, I'm afraid you are one of the jerks. Any tendency toward social quadriplegia will make you a washout at Hedo, where your wits and charm carry you more than your looks, wallet, or business acumen.

Always bring a drink or two with you to the hot tub.

Don't do the trapeze after being in water all day. Your skin will be too soft and rip easily.

When you finish packing, remove half the clothing from your suitcase. Hedo is casual and you can wear beachwear everywhere, except Pastafari, where shoes are required.

Watch for "tile comet" before heading to the nude beach from your room. The beach crowd might not inform you of the toilet paper stuck to your butt or heel because they are laughing too loud. One year, a man made a Pyjama night costume by sticking a wad of toilet paper in his butt and went like that to the disco.

What you might not know to pack

Batteries for your camera or video camera

Film (too pricey at Hedo) I use one roll a week, but even some regulars go through a roll a day.

Inflatable raft *(See Chapter 3, Bring Your Own Raft.)*

Waterproof marker to label raft as yours

Items to trade for services with locals (shoe polish for wood carvers)

Medicine, tweezers (Benedryl, Cortaid, and Band-Aids)

Bug killer (sand fleas at dusk can be nasty)

Lysol spray for the mold in the air conditioners

Key holder, unless you prefer Hedo's elastic band

Business or address cards to share with new friends

Flashlight for the room—to find the candle and matches (for the occasional power outage)

Hangers (closets have five or six per person)

Thumbtacks or tape for attaching signs to doors

Travel clock

Two pairs of sunglasses (you will lose the first pair)

Eyeglass strap (if you bring one pair)

Toys: Silly String, confetti, stickers, tub floats

Shaving cream for a tour of Sandals

Edible body paints

Butter salt to add to popcorn on the beach

Chalk to write on boards or pavement

Paint brushes for body painting—Hedo's are sometimes nonexistent or limited, but fingers are fun too

Spa Scents to make the hot tub smell good

Undies to wear down and a pair to wear back home

Hat with a long bill that can withstand sun and rain (for standing in the hot tub during downpours)

Large, insulated mug with a cover and a straw so Delroy can mix you a triple, and you can stay in the ocean longer (cover keeps rain and popcorn out of it)

CDs or tapes for the player in your room

Quart-size zip-lock-type plastic bags for keeping cigarettes, drugs, and sundries dry in on the beach and in the hot tub. Also for packing a meal for the return trip to MoBay.

Belt and safety pins for creating your toga

Water shoes to protect your feet from rocks and sea urchins

Cigarettes, bring your own. Nasty brands are sold at the store but they frequently run out. Hedo no longer provides free cigarettes on the bar.

Good attitude and an open mind

Do I need to bring money?

Bring at least 10 $1 bills for tipping luggage porters at the airport ($1 per bag per person who touches it). Tips are not given at the resort, but never has anyone turned down cash. Just do it in a way that's secret because the staff can lose their job by accepting money from you. Gifts make great tips.

Bring only the new big Ben head $100 bills; some places won't accept the old ones. Store clerks often use iodine on U.S. currency to test for counterfeits.

At Hedo, a massage on the beach will cost you $50 or so depending on going rate and tip. If you want Rosie to braid your chest hair, that'll cost cash. Wood carvings and names or initials engraved in dead trees cost bucks too. The Hedo boutique, jewelry, and sundries stores take credit cards.

U.S. dollars are desired everywhere, but you're likely to receive Jamaican dollars for change. Hedo has a money exchange in the main lobby. If you do exchange U.S. money for Jamaican, save the receipt for later exchange to U.S. money. The J next to a dollar amount on an item means Jamaican dollar.

The airport departure tax is $500 J or $15 U.S. Some charter flights include the tax in the air fare.

Why people go to Hedo

"We go to Hedo because we can live out any fantasy we have or have thought we wanted to have. We also have such great friends we meet year after year. There's crazy, zany behavior; sexual behavior; and honesty. Hedo is like coming home to a place away from home."

—California girl

"Hedo gives you the freedom of not having to wear clothes. You also meet marvelous, open-minded people there; we've met many friends we've stayed in touch with. It's a total break from the rigid day-to-day routine of my office and provides me a natural high and many laughs."

—Marian from Pennsylvania

"Hedo is a place where the strangers really are just friends you haven't met yet. You can have good clean fun, naked, with a lot of really fun caring people. You can also be as nasty as you wanna be."

—Orgasmic in Oregon

"Hedo is an adult Disney World. We went to Disney World seven times then found out about Hedo. Never been back to Mickey's world but have returned to Hedo 16 times. I guess because you get to act goofy there."

—Bill and Jo Anne from New Jersey

"Hedo is the only place you can escape to and be whoever or whatever you want to be with no worries or thoughts about reality."

—Millie from New York, married, age 53

"I never laugh as much as when I am at Hedo. And the sex is great too."

—Slinky from the South a.k.a. Bookie

"I've been coming to Hedo for 13 years. I come for the sun, the sand, the ganja, and, most importantly, my friends. I've met so many wonderful people through the years. I can travel to any big city in the U.S.A. or Europe and know somebody who I met at Hedo."

—Jennifer from Cleveland, married, age 42

"Being at Hedo is similar to attending a major spectator sporting event rather than watching it on TV. You get to experience the equivalent of the noise, the fan fights, barfing beer drinkers, others carrying out their fantasies (maybe yours too)."

—Bill Schwemer from Virginia, married, age 57

"I have met the best friends of my life in Hedo. I am filled with warm, pleasant thoughts every time I think of Hedo. Even though I'm not from the United States, where the majority of people in Hedo come from, I find I'm communicating with at least 15 people year round.

My husband and I find Hedo is a place where you can truly be yourself and enjoy yourself without causing friction to your partner, unless of course, it's the right type of friction! We have had wonderful shared experiences, both physically and mentally. Mostly the hilarity of occasions among friends indelibly printed in our memory keeps bringing us back."

—Across the Atlantic: the babe who gave a blow job
to the blow-up doll in the nude pool
and received a standing ovation.

Chapter 2

The lay of the land

Hedo started as Negril Beach Village in 1976. The 70s were turbulent political times in Jamaica, so the government finished building the hotel and took over its management from the Issa family. By 1981, John Issa had formed SuperClubs and regained management control of the hotel. SuperClubs renamed the hotel Hedonism II to retain the connection with the original hotel (which had used *hedonism* as its motto) but show that management had changed. "Hedonism I" never existed. Hedonism III in Runaway Bay is scheduled to open late 1999.

First there was the bus. And it was evil.

Cow, goat, shack, cow, goat, shack, cow, goat, shack.

Some call the 1½-hour bus ride to Hedo from Sangster International Airport in MoBay "The Bus Ride from Hell." People have T-shirts that read "I survived the road to Negril."

If everyone on the bus is going to Hedo (not the norm anymore), the ride has a party atmosphere, providing a head start on the vacation. Sometimes the bus stops for cold beer halfway along the miserable potholed asphalt the Jamaicans call a road, but you can load up at the airport too. The bus seldom takes off within 20 minutes of your arrival to the airport, so be patient.

All first-timers to Jamaica should take the bus for the experience. The ride lets you see roadside Jamaica—lots of lush greenery, bony farm animals, and brightly painted shanties with aluminum roofs. Always ask permission to take someone's photograph as a courtesy.

Many of the homes you see on the edge of the road are on government property. People are allowed to live there because of the trouble of moving them. Many use battery-powered radios to find out what's going on because phones are costly. You might be surprised to hear obituaries on the radio.

Jamaica is an impoverished, but proud nation. The ride depresses some people. The Jockey Underwear factory along Manley Boulevard is the high point of the ride.

The wealthy aren't visible from the street. Their opulent concrete homes nestle in the hills, and they enjoy spectacular views of the ocean.

If you stop, children and adults beg from you. If you want to make a contribution to Jamaica, though, ask at the hotel front desk regarding the many schools that desperately need donations—especially schools for young boys, who often have to make their way through life on their own because their parents can't care for them. Many Hedo guests make regular donations, but rarely does anyone at Hedo ask first.

Spend a buck or two for the sugar cane sold on the side of the road. A little goes a long way to share on the bus. Bite and suck on the sweetness. Spit out the parts that don't chew easily.

You may see high hills, but these hills are not the Blue Mountains where Jamaica grows its renowned coffee. Those mountains are well on the other side of the island, which is on the whole roughly 100 miles east to west and 50 miles north to south. Negril is about 90 miles south of Cuba.

The roads are asphalt, bumpy, and winding on the way to Negril. Although Negril is closer to MoBay than Ocho Rios is, the ride is as long because of the curves. If you are susceptible to car sickness, you may purge yourself of evil spirits. Just let the bus driver know, so you can hop out into the grass.

If you take the bus ride back to MoBay you usually leave Hedo three hours before your scheduled flight for the hotel to take responsibility for a missed flight. If you miss your scheduled bus departure, you can take the next one, but leaving Hedo only two hours ahead of departure is cutting it close. Most people take the bus—its cost is included in the hotel rate.

God invented Cessnas. And they were good.

Three airlines can shuttle you from MoBay to Negril on a 17-minute flight. The flight presents breathtaking views of the coral reefs and water, and best of all you beat the bus so you have a smaller crowd at check-in.

Many flights are four-seater Cessnas. Three people plus the pilot can ride comfortably. Five passengers have been squished in, but sometimes the luggage doesn't fit and is sent later.

The one-way price is about $130 for one, $60 each for two, and $50 each for three. Credit card payment is 5% extra. Sometimes reserved round-trip rates are $250 for two. Aero

Express offers about eight daily scheduled flights each way at slightly lower rates.

I travel alone and never book a flight in advance when I arrive in MoBay. I just ask who's leaving next and go on that charter, usually with another couple. Always make sure to reserve a flight back to MoBay though, especially if you returning on a weekend, when flights are harder to come by. Rarely are flights at night because the Greater Negril Aero Terminal (GNAT) has no runway lights.

If you show up by yourself and don't want to pay the $130 one-way fare, tell the ticket agent you'll wait for the next flight —one is always leaving within a half hour, which is always better for speed and comfort than the bus. If the flight is just returning to Negril empty for a pickup in Negril, don't let the airline charge you the full $130 fare. If they went without you, no fare would be paid for that leg of the trip.

Air Negril, Aero Express, and TimAir have no discernible differences. Each has friendly staffs, similar prices, and charter service to take you where you want to go and usually when you want to go too.

Often they meet you outside customs in MoBay and put you in a cab for the three-minute ride to the other side of the airport where the old charter terminal is. They pay for the cab; you pay the baggage tip.

Tip $1 per bag per each person who touches them, but condoms work just as well in many cases. (Condoms are costly in Jamaica.) Tip the pilot $5 if he buzzes the Hedo nude beach, which some claim isn't permitted anymore.

For a return flight, call one of the three charter airlines (list in back of book). Or take the five-minute stroll to the GNAT. Turn left outside the resort, back toward MoBay. Go past the T-shirt stalls and cross the street at the airport sign. The shacks at the airport house some of the airline's ticket agents. Give a credit card number to hold the reservation. You can pay for the flight in cash when you take it to avoid the 5% surcharge, if you like.

The walk over to the airport is short and safe, but women will likely have to tell men to go away during the trek. You can shop the ever-exclusive stalls of Rodeo Drive on the way back, too, but remember to bargain for the best deals on T-shirts and small wooden statues.

By flying out you can stay at the resort longer since you don't have the long bus ride. For example, a 3 p.m. departure from MoBay means you leave Hedo at 11 a.m. by bus. If you take a flight, you leave around 1:15 p.m., which means you enjoyed lunch and had a slow, relaxing morning.

Hedo provides a free taxi ride to and from GNAT; just nicely remind the cab driver to avoid paying the $5 fare. Do tip him $1 per bag, though.

Call the airlines direct to reserve, or go through your travel agent and possibly pay more. See the end of the book for phone numbers.

Check-in is tedious; check-out a breeze

A three-man band plays old island tunes as buses and taxis pull up to the front desk. Sometimes an entertainment coordinator greets guests with champagne.

Patience is key when checking in to Hedo. In Jamaica patience is an art form. On return to the United States you'll wait inordinate amounts of time while your friends tap their feet in anger. Island time ("soon come, mon") is not a bad thing.

The check-in process can take 20 minutes even if you are first in line. Although the hotel has computers, they are not used for check-in. Your name should appear on the front desk's typed sheet (possibly under layers of White-Out or erased pencil marks).

The nude swimming pool complex has a swim-up bar, where you can see the beach beyond.

If many people are at check-in, just leave your luggage (not your money) at the front desk and head to the bar for an adult beverage. (The minute you make it past the chain at the outer gate, you are a guest of the hotel.) You are likely in street clothes and warm. The drink takes the traveling edge off.

Sometimes Hedo has a room assigned when you arrive (supposedly based on what you bought) but sometimes it doesn't. And if the rooms aren't fully booked (the staff always says they are), then you can ask for specific rooms or locations.

Some people ask for a specific room number and actually get it (often they faxed their request the week before). These are privileged people. Most take what they can and try to change it later if it's not their choice. *(See: Types of Rooms To Choose.)*

Some people pay for a nude beach-view room and end up with a less costly nude garden, or even a room on the prude side. Hedo hasn't been refunding the difference in money but instead provides free nights for your return trip to Hedo. The use of those complimentary nights has limitations, so be diligent to ensure the free nights are something you can use with your schedule. Everything is negotiable.

If you want to upgrade your room when you arrive, you'll not likely be able to when the resort is packed, which is from late October through May.

Sometimes you'll arrive and have to stay at the Point Village next door because Hedo has overbooked. This is a minor hardship, but some people get mad and complain with various levels of success to the hotel. During busy season, avoid arriving late on a Saturday, or the odds are high Hedo will send you next door. Hedo pays for your cab back and forth, or you can walk the short distance.

Weekends socially are slower than weekdays because of the huge numbers of people arriving and leaving. The friend you make on Saturday is likely gone Sunday. You once could tell the newcomers by their white skin, but that's changing as more people use SPF 30 and stay under the trees.

At check-in you receive two keys. One for your room (remember your room number) and one for the safe in the closet for your valuables. The room key is easily replaced, but the safe key is not. A lost safe key costs $50 to replace. A staff member is happy to walk you to your room. Your heavy luggage might be sent later.

The day before you leave, the depression starts when you receive the dreaded eviction notice under your door. This sheet of paper lists when your bus and flight home leaves.

Although you must check out by noon, you can always keep your bags in a friend's room and clean up there.

Check-out is glorious—drop off the keys on the front desk and leave. You can complete the opinion form found on the front desk in advance on the beach with your friends, where you'll remember all the good, bad, and ugly details better.

Rooms are for sex and sleeping only

The old swinger story that has also circulated at Hedo for years was that swinger women would throw their keys into a pile, and the men would pick one and go to that room to be with whomever they got. Though the truth of this event has never been confirmed or denied, you can seldom doubt even the most exotic tales told about the place having happened there at least once. But they can't play that particular game anymore because the room keys no longer have the room number on them.

This lack of room number can make finding your room difficult. But Keith from Pennsylvania has perfected a way to hone in on his room. He lights the entire vicinity of his room with Christmas lights and flags as markers. But he admitted even that didn't help once, and he slept in the bushes one night.

What to expect in the rooms

Most people spend little time in their rooms because sleeping at Hedo seems to be a complete waste of time.

Don't look for Gideon bibles in the drawers; you'll only find paper-wrapped candles. One couple found the candles and asked, "How did the hotel know we liked flicking wax on each other?" The candles are for the occasional blackout. Nowadays, though, the power outages only last a few moments.

The Tropics sport big roaches (both kinds) and bats too, but not as daily visitors. Sometimes a crab (of the crustaceous variety) greets you at your door and waggles its claws menacingly before clopping off sideways.

The morning sun comes in the windows and under the door (reflecting off that white tile floor) mighty early and mighty bright. One friend brings masking tape to seal the drapes to the wall to keep the room dark. Abscond with extra beach towels to use as carpeting because those tile floors are cold and slippery when wet.

If the air-conditioning is strong, leave it on during the day and shut it off at night so you don't suffer a sore throat. (The nonstop talking, yelling, and singing in the piano bar does that by itself.) Some people bring Lysol spray to disinfect the unit's filters.

If your toilet has been acting up, flush before you poop to ensure it is still working. And beware of flushing toilets, they can affect pressure and temperature of the showers. Actually any toilet flushed in the building seems to affect the pressure and temperature. Most claim any toilet in Negril causes the same effect.

When single guys complain about the cold showers tell them the hotel purposefully provides cold showers especially for them because of the lack of single women. For hot water, go to the hot tub. Most guests experience latherphobia at Hedo (the fear of the hot water running out just after soaping up).

Overall, the pressure and water temperature in most of the rooms, most of the time, is satisfactory but rarely excellent. Just don't expect a shower between 6 and 7:30 p.m.—when everyone is showering—to be a pleasant experience.

The tap water in Jamaica is good and safe to drink. The maid fills the brown pitcher in your room with ice each day. I had been going to Hedo for 10 years before I noticed.

Alarm clocks are missing from most rooms so bring one or rely on the not-always-reliable wake-up call from the hotel. The rooms have dressers and nightstands with a total of 10 drawers, a hanging wardrobe with 10 to 12 wooden hangers and a key-lock safe, an ironing board and iron, and beach and bath towels. If the ironing board keeps falling on your head when you open the door, put it under your bed. One guest ended up with five boards under his bed because the maid kept replacing them.

Check the chain lock on your door. Some were installed backward so the chain falls out when the door opens. No smoke detectors are in the rooms. Guests have brought their own.

The blow dryers on the bathroom wall usually work and are pleasant for drying recently washed pubic hair—if you have it; on the nude beach some people don't.

The CD-cassette-player-radio works, but remember that most of them are plugged into a socket that only works if you turn on the light switch on the wall.

Speaking of light switches, the bathroom light is not in the bathroom, but on the wall outside it. Memorize which one it is so you don't flip them all at night and disturb your sleeping roommate.

Some people bring light bulbs because the bulbs in the room, although the environmentally friendly type, are not bright. The bathroom is bright enough for applying makeup.

Outlets are wired for 110V, 50 cycles instead of 60 cycles as in the United States. This wreaks havoc with plug-in marital aids. That's why they make a funny whining sound and are not as powerful as at home. My friend Teresa no longer invites Vicki the vibrator to Hedo for this reason. And remember to bring lots of batteries for nonelectric models. C batteries are hard to find, and all batteries are costly in Jamaica. This 50-cycle system also affects some clocks' accuracy. Electric gadgets plug in without special adapters, though.

Rumor has it some people have used the coffee makers in the room, but most prefer the socialization of the dining area or beach for their morning java fix.

If you don't have a blanket on your bed, ask the maid for one, just in case. Also ask for extra pillows because the quality varies and then you can have your choice.

The ceilings sport large, sometimes funhouse-like mirrors. Stay out of the fat part of the mirror when making love. Be wary of men always looking for the long part of the mirror.

You can also see yourself in the big wall mirror if you are on the bed on your knees.

Hedo has no balconies for its rooms. But the windows are big, so leave the lights on and enjoy yourselves on the padded build-in sofa at the window; people are happy to watch as they troll the beach at night. *(See Chapter 4: Voyeurism and Exhibitionism: The Hedo Way of Life.)*

Types of rooms to choose

Hedo has 280 guest rooms, all air-conditioned with private bathrooms. All rooms look the same and have either two twin beds or a king-size bed. Mattresses are firm, usually because a board is under them.

Beware of king-size beds that are really two twins...one swinging foursome lost a girl when the beds suddenly separated. You often must request a king-size bed at check-in to get one. The maid also can arrange one but not usually right away.

Tales from the Naked City

One day at lunch, two 40-ish ladies, who are still in what would be considered street clothes at Hedo, joined a man in his swimsuit, who was seated. They had arrived only about an hour before. He asked the usual name, where you are from, and then asked what they liked so far. The reply in a taken aback and shocked manner was, "We got to our room and opened the drapes, and there were naked people outside the window." He replied, "Oh, you got one of the good rooms," and he walked away for a second course, showing the back of his thong swimsuit.

If you want a specific room, you can only get it if it is available and you are special enough. Rooms starting with a 21 or 22 are nude-side rooms. If the room number starts with 11 or 12, it is a prude-side room. Sex is permitted in all rooms.

When you book a room, you choose from four types of room locations, which determines the price you pay. Before 1997, Hedo priced all its rooms the same. On average, and depending on season and room location, a night at Hedo costs $200 U.S.

Nude beach: 70 rooms; most costly and highly desired. Water pressure problems are slightly more notorious in these rooms than others. Trees might block the beach view. Privacy is limited on the first floor in the higher-numbered rooms because crowds of beach people can see you unless you draw the drapes, thus losing the point of having a beach view. But then again, naked people are not always shy or private.

If you want nude beach views, ask for Room 2116 (or second-floor Room 2216) or larger to be away from the disco and have the potential for a decent ocean view. Rooms 2175 to 2180 and its second-floor counterparts, Rooms 2275 to 2280, are loud during the day and can be loud at night because they're so close to the hot tub. Rooms 2180 and 2280 are right next to the nude pool complex.

Nude garden: 60 rooms: second most costly and also desired by Nudes. You can choose from the H-block or basketball court rooms. The H-block, so named for the shape all the rooms form, can be extremely quiet or noisy depending on who's there. These rooms are ideal because they are not too far or too close to anything. Some claim the basketball court rooms are too noisy because of the bouncing ball, but that's not a constant or a guaranteed problem.

Rooms 2134 to 2150 and 2234 to 2250 are H-block rooms. Rooms 2151 to 2165 and 2251 to 2265 are basketball court rooms.

Prude beach: 60 rooms: These third most costly rooms, with pretty views of the beach, result in a six-minute walk to the nude beach via the prude beach. These rooms are close to the disco: Rooms 1101 to 1110 and Rooms 1201 to 1210.

Prude garden: 90 rooms. Least costly; no one wants them unless they are die-hard Prudes and just don't want to look at the ocean while sitting on the toilet.

In any of the rooms, if you are on the first floor, you can hear a person on the second floor above drop a button on the tile floor, which is nothing compared with the torture of the stool being dragged across the floor. Friends living above other friends often antagonize one another this way.

Advantage of first-floor rooms:

• No stairs to climb: fast, easy access.

Advantage of second-floor rooms:

• Quieter
• Less likely to have theft or voyeurs
• Can comfortably leave window open while sleeping
• Better view of ocean if oceanfront

To get an ocean view without paying for it, ask for a second-floor nude rooms next to the basketball court. They often have an ocean view over the rooftops of the actual ocean-view rooms.

Stay away from the disco and hot tub for more quiet

The thump-thump of the disco isn't as bad as people say, unless you are sensitive. The reverb on the stucco buildings from door slamming is more likely to cause sudden lurches from slumber. Generally, to avoid the disco sounds, ask for a room with a big number. These prude garden rooms also are close to the disco: Rooms 1131 to 1135 and Rooms 1231 to 1235.

The best rooms for quiet on the nude side is 2150 or 2250 in the H-block and 2165, but it's off the basketball courts, which isn't everyone's main choice because of the erstwhile irritating game.

Keep your room quiet by closing the bathroom window louvers and the bathroom door—makes a difference on keeping the room comfortable in temperature too.

Tales from the Naked City

The rain had infested the entire afternoon and everyone had already indulged in the 3Ss: sex, sensimilla, and sleep, so a new activity was needed. About 100 of us knew each other so we started hanging out on the second floor to party à la college dorm style, going from room to room along the outdoor walkways. People filled their water pitchers with beer and shared.

At the second-floor bridge that connects the nude beach rooms to the H-block rooms, the party turned into a photo op. Everyone hung their butt over the railing on the bridge; first girls, then guys. The girls did breasts. When the guys did peckers, though, Joe figured he had to pee—right off the side of the walkway bridge.

Should I get a roommate?

If you are single, you can have a same-sex roommate assigned, bring your own roommate, or pay $100 extra per night to have your own room. General rule: if you have money to burn, get a single. If you are male traveling alone, get a single.

The front desk might ask if you want a smoking or nonsmoking roommate, but your answer has no bearing on which you might actually end up with.

The sex of your roommate usually matches your own, but I've been assigned a male roommate twice. And one was especially handsome and charming, but another woman

34

snapped him up before I could catch him. (In Jamaica, Chris is a man's name, not usually a woman's.)

Women tend to share rooms. The arrangement usually works fine or makes for good stories. Women also respect and appreciate when a single man has his own room, but single men can successfully share with an assigned stranger and keep costs down.

Male roommates tend to be ruder than female ones and have been known to lock out roommates. One male friend tells of an assigned roommate who insisted on marking his side of the room with masking tape. The front desk helps you switch rooms at a moment's notice whenever possible.

Tales from the Naked City

I had a single-share room with a stranger. Everything went fine until the second night. I came in at about 2 a.m. from Veronica's and had to pee real bad. The room light was on so I knocked on the bathroom door. No answer. So I tried to open the door. Something blocked it. At first I thought the bath mat was in the way so I pushed harder. When I could get my head in I saw my roomie lying on the floor. I thought he had fallen or had a heart attack, so I gave the door a good push and entered. He woke up and looked up at me and said, "Please don't unlock me. I don't want to fall off the Earth." He was handcuffed around the toilet bowl. Seems he was doing a few of the island chemicals and wigged out.

Last year I was relating this experience to some people at dinner. I said, "Can you believe bringing handcuffs to Hedo?" With that, I hear four clanging sounds as four sets of handcuffs hit the table. One pair was furry.

—Bob "Studman" Starz from New Jersey, age 58.
"Studman" is a business name not a sexual prowess.

People are never serious with inflatable toys on the nude beach.

How to use the telephones

The phones are not as intrusive as guests thought they would be when Hedo wired the rooms in 1997. They unplug too. The phones help for quickly arranging dinner or toga-tying plans with friends, reaching the front desk, or making reservations for the on-campus Italian restaurant, Pastafari. The front lobby also has phones.

To make an outside call, set up an account at the front desk first. Billing long-distance calls to your room is often $10 or more per minute.

Ignore the instructions on the card by the phone. They do not work. Before you go to Hedo, call your long-distance carrier and ask for the best way to call from Jamaica.

AT&T calling procedure:

1. Get an outside line (operator will tell you, if you can reach the operator).
2. Dial 872 (country code for Jamaica).
3. Dial area code + phone number.
4. Enter AT&T account number and PIN.

An outside line isn't always available, so you can call collect, which some sources say is cheaper than using an outside line:

1. Dial 0.
2. Dial 800-872-2881 (AT&T's toll-free number to the United States).
3. Dial 1 + area code + phone number.

Phones dial long distance but sometimes phone cards have blocks on them per the Jamaican telephone company, which was apparently getting burned with stolen cards. One guest tried three MCI, two AT&T, and three credit cards and was not able to make a call.

Another trick is to call the States collect when the lines aren't busy (which is rare) and have the person refuse the charge. The person in the States then knows to call you immediately. For incoming international calls, the room phone system is fine. The hotel gives the caller the correct room for the first call. After that, callers can ask for the room number.

If you are at one of the bars waiting incessantly for a friend, ask the bartenders if you can use the bar phone to call your buddy. They'll let you—but be quick and polite to avoid abusing this privilege.

Setting up a cell phone account in Jamaica is a long, difficult process, I've been told. On arrival in Jamaica ask TOJ (Telecommunications of Jamaica) to set up an account for about $50 U.S. Then calls are a buck or so a minute, according to reports. The cell phone must be programmed with TOJ's number to receive calls. Cell sites are prevalent.

You can receive faxes at Hedo. The staff will find you. Some guests politely ask to use the hotel fax to send information back to the States.

Finding a boob-tube fix

The rooms at Hedo do not have televisions, but you can watch shows in the TV room near Veronica's piano bar and the big chess set. Hedo has a satellite dish and receives most sports and commercial broadcasts from the United States, including HBO. CNN is usually on all day long.

Guests can control the lights in the room, and the windows are blacked out so you can't see in or out. Many guests don't even realize this air-conditioned, seldom-used facility of the hotel is even there. Rumors are sprouting up about its use as a make-out pit, which the piano bar used to be before the hotel started locking it up after 2 a.m.

TVs are available outside Hedo too. Take a ride or walk south on the beach to Margueritaville, a beach sports bar just past Negril Tree House, with its excellent large-screen TVs. Other bars, such as Rick's, also have TVs.

The grotto, nicknamed the fornicatorium, here without its waterfall drape, fits more than 45 people—quite tightly—six comfortably. The misting pool with its center fountain bidet (not operating here) becomes the seating for the show.

Meals are relentless like on a docked cruise ship

Food at Hedo becomes a big focus of the day. For shear volume, the 500 or so guests at the hotel inhale prodigious quantities: Each day Hedo guests consume 14 pounds of salt and 1,600 eggs.

Tales from the Naked City

A couple sat on the lounges behind me at the beach. The man leaned over to his girlfriend and said, "Well, honey, what do you think? Should we go up to the dining room and have lunch—or should we just stay here and have another drink?" That was likely the most difficult decision they made during their entire stay at Hedo.

—John of Palm Springs, Calif.

No one starves at Hedo. That span between 10:30 a.m. and noon is rough, though, because no food is served. Alcohol is served, however, and can be used to bump caloric intake should faintness occur from a sugar low. One dirty banana drink is equivalent to two meals.

Breakfast, lunch, and dinner are served buffet style in an open-air but roofed dining area. In the dead of summer, seek a seat under a moving fan to avoid dripping on your meal.

The dining area has cloth seat cushions that don't imprint your naked butt when wearing a thong, short skirt, or revealing toga, but sit on a towel. The staff prefers you don't use the napkins under your butt and readily brings a beach towel to sit on.

The chairs are slightly low in the main dining area and best for lounging rather than eating. In the Pastafari restaurant, chairs are a more civilized height, keeping faces farther from plates.

- Breakfast runs 8:00 a.m. to 10:30 a.m.
- Lunch runs 12:30 p.m. to 3:00 p.m.
- Dinner runs 7:30 p.m. to 10:00 p.m.

Hedo offers food at many times of day and night at other locations:

Coffee and either fruit or cookies and muffins are available at Delroy's (bar on the nude beach) each morning around 7.

Cocktail appetizers usually are served somewhere on the prude side around 6-ish.

Midnight snack is from midnight to 1:00 a.m.

Breakfast and lunch are often better than dinner. Salad is always fine. Soups are excellent. A friend tells me Jamaicans use edible wax as filler in the cheese, but I haven't confirmed this rumor. It's good; I eat it anyway.

Dinner guests also can eat at the air-conditioned Pastafari Italian Restaurant (nicknamed RastaPasta) 6:30 p.m. to 1 a.m. Make reservations at the front desk to guarantee seating, especially for groups larger than four or on Wednesday's detested Chinese night. Pastafari is not open Thursday, Toga night.

Pastafari, which requires guests to wear shoes, is excellent when it's good and pitiful when it's not. But the champagne and quiet music there make up for any evils. Eating there instead of the midnight buffet is a treat. The menu in Pastafari changes twice a week now. It offers fresh fish and seafood every day, but the variety in meat dishes is dwindling. After 10 p.m., you can only order pasta. The antipasto bar in the Pastafari is tasty, sometimes with chilled mussels.

Tales from the Naked City

When the Jamaican cook asked the young Hedo guest if he wanted any jerk chicken, the young man responded, "No, not if it's defective."

Two beach grills are available, one located on the prude beach and one on the nude beach. Both open at noon. The nude beach grill closes at 11 p.m.

Robert's sandwiches at the nude beach grill are well-loved by all, and sometimes at night you can find incredible jerk chicken or freshly grilled fish to eat with your fingers that more than pleases the palate. You can sit in the hot tub eating jerk chicken and sucking on a Dirty Banana. Life seldom gets better.

Lobster at Hedo is sometimes plentiful; other times not seen—depends on season and distributor. The Negril marine conservation authorities generally close the lobster season April 1 through June 30.

Bring the flavor of Jamaica home

Robert, the head cook at the nude beach grill, is one of Hedo's premier chefs. Here is his recipe for the best jerk sauce.

Robert Kerr's Authentic Jamaican Jerk Sauce:

1 10 oz. bottle of soy sauce (low sodium is best)

1 10 oz. bottle of Pickapeppa Sauce (look near A-1 in a grocery store)

1 5 oz. or 10 oz. bottle of Tabasco (or Grace Brand Hot Pepper Sauce)

2 tbs. Cajun seasoning (any kind)

2 tsp. black pepper

1 bunch of scallions—well chopped

1 large onion—well chopped

1 tbs. fresh thyme

1 tsp. ground cinnamon

1 tbs. Jamaican allspice (a.k.a. ground pimento)

1 oz. hickory "liquid smoke" (at the grocery store)

Mix all liquids together and then add the spices, etc. Let sauce marinade over meat in covered container overnight in refrigerator. Slow cook two pounds of chicken or pork over low to medium heat—basting with extra sauce till done.

Place a drippings pan under cooking meat to catch runoff. Remove drippings pan and add Red Stripe beer (room temperature) or your brand for a dipping sauce. A squirt of fresh lime juice over the meat adds a nice touch before tasting.

Can I buy you a drink?

Alcohol flows freely at Hedo, especially since it's included in your package cost, but most people handle their drinking well. The occasional youngster passes out, so the staff loads him on a beach chair and carries him to his room. If the boy was belligerent on the way to passing out, the hotel may post a guard at the door to make sure he doesn't escape.

On average each day at Hedo, guests drink 57 bottles of rum, 45 bottles of vodka, and 21 tanks of beer. And that doesn't include all the other types of booze pulled through a straw. The hotel estimates only three bottles of rum, two bottles of vodka, and one-and-a half tanks of beer of those totals are ordered but not consumed.

All five bars at Hedo are well stocked, but Veronica's piano bar has the best call brands. The bartenders don't make blender drinks there, though.

Main dining area bar: 10 a.m. to 1 a.m.

Prude beach bar: 10 a.m. to 5 p.m.

Nude beach bar: 10 a.m. to 11 p.m.

Piano bar: 6 p.m. to 2 a.m.

Disco bar: 11 p.m. to 5 a.m., or until the last guest leaves

Finding booze from 5 a.m. to 10 a.m. is tricky. Try bribing the night staff to bring you beer. Or check the tap at the old Delroy's beach bar. Sometimes beer is still there.

Beer drinkers better enjoy Red Stripe. That's all the beer Hedo serves. If you are friends with Matt the Mayor, a regular guest, he'll likely share his garbage can full of iced Heineken with you.

To keep the Red Stripe cold, many drink it on ice. Or ask for a Shandy Draft, which is beer on ice with a ginger ale topper (sometimes up to half). The ginger ale in Jamaica is kickier than at home and cuts the bitter of the beer to create a drinkable beverage. In Europe, sometimes lemonade replaces ginger ale for this drink.

Rainy afternoons often produce clusters of guests in the hot tub wearing hats and carrying covered drinks. The expression "Bleaky Day, Soon Turn Drunk" describes it all.

Tales from the Naked City

The iced tea here has too much booze in it. *Overheard from a dizzy girl after her drink order at the bar.*

If you stick with one drink and are pleasant, the bartender sometimes prepares it automatically when you step up to the bar. Hedo's bartenders are sharp.

If you need booze for the hot tub late at night, pick up large quantities of it at the main bar before it closes at 1 a.m. or at Veronica's before 2 a.m. If you wait to hit the disco bar, you can only receive one drink at a time.

The flaming Bob Marley shot is evil and colorful with its strawberry syrup, crème de menthe, rum, and overproof rum layers of booze representing Jamaica's colors.

Tia Maria is the Jamaica version of Kahlua, a coffee-flavored liqueur. On ice, Tia is a pleasant after-dinner drink. All veterans have at least four bottles of Tia at home, won in past competitions when bottles of booze were prizes.

If you want a change from alcoholic drinks, ask the bartender for Ting, a refreshing grapefruit soda, similar to Fresca, available all over Jamaica. The fresh-squeezed grapefruit juice at the bar also mixes well with club soda for a light drink.

Make Hedo drinks at home

At the main bar plaques describe the many island mixed drinks. Some young men and women make their mission to have one of each in a single night.

Although the drinks never taste the same, many people want to try making them at home. You can buy a common brand name of bar syrup, but you also can make it yourself. To make simple syrup, mix ½ cup sugar with ½ cup water and bring to a rapid boil. Simmer for a minute or two and let cool. Makes ¾ cup syrup.

VODKA SLUSH
(When tapping on the bottom
of your glass to reach the last
bit, it falls on your face.)
1 oz. vodka
1 oz. lime juice
1 oz. simple syrup
Add ice and blend.

MUDSLIDE
1½ oz. Bailey's
½ oz. Tia Maria
1½ oz. vodka
Add ice and blend.

DIRTY BANANA
1 medium banana
1 to 1½ oz. Tia Maria
Table sugar (to taste)
Milk or cream
Add ice and blend.

JAMAICAN RUM PUNCH
1 oz. light rum
1 oz. overproof rum
2 oz. pineapple juice
2 oz. orange juice
2 oz. lime juice
Strawberry syrup to taste

PURPLE RAIN
1 oz. vodka
¼ to ½ oz. blue curacao
¼ to ½ oz. grenadine
1 oz. fruit syrup
¼ to ½ oz. lime juice
Add ice and blend.

GREEN GRASS
OF HOME
1 oz. Appleton white rum
2 oz. orange juice
¼ oz. blue curacao
¼ oz. lime juice
Add ice and blend.

LAND SHARK
¼ oz. peach schnapps
1 oz. vodka
¼ oz. strawberry syrup
1 oz. orange juice
¼ oz. lime juice
Pour over ice.

HUMMINGBIRD
1 medium banana
1 oz. Tia Maria
1 oz. rum cream liqueur
1 oz. vodka
Strawberry syrup
Milk or cream
Add ice and blend.

BIG BAMBOO
1 oz. overproof rum
1 oz. light rum
½ oz. triple sec
1 oz. pineapple juice
1 oz. orange juice
1 oz. lime juice
¾ oz. syrup
Pour over ice.

NEGRIL STINGER
1 oz. gold rum
½ oz. Tia Maria

JAMAICAN KISS
1 oz. Tia Maria
1 oz. light rum
1 tbs. cream

NO PROBLEM
1 oz. coconut rum
¾ oz. crème de banana
½ oz. lime juice
½ oz. fruit juice
1 oz. pineapple juice
1 oz. grapefruit juice
1 oz. orange juice

BUTTERY NIPPLE SHOT
½ Bailey's Irish Cream
½ butterscotch schnapps

SLIPPERY NIPPLE SHOT
1/3 Bailey's
1/3 schnapps
1/3 vodka
ALSO:
50/50 Bailey's and
Sambuka.
—Only for drinking off
specified body part.

Hedo rules are few

Rule #1: If you are going to the bar, ask if anyone else wants a drink too. You don't actually have to bring the person's drink back, though, because a million excuses could befall you along the way.

The glory of Hedo is its lack of rules found at home. But Hedo itself does have three rules:

- Do not bring glass to the beach or pool areas.
- Do not dress inappropriately (too many or too few clothes) for the area of the hotel you are in.
- Do not perform sexual acts in public places.

The nude beach signs say "No Photography," but that's not always applicable.

> "Hedo is a place as well as a state of mind, where you walk through the front lobby, and walk out of your everyday life into a parallel universe where none of the regular rules apply. This doesn't mean that no rules apply—just that the regular 'walk, don't walk,' 'don't take off your clothes in public,' 'don't drink before 5 p.m.,' 'don't eat fatty foods' rules don't apply. Paradoxically, giving people complete freedom to do what they will imposes a lot of responsibility. And a new set of rules, for the most part self-imposed, comes into play."
> —Parfumier (formerly on AOL)

Hedo is a no-holds-barred place, but it does have a unique decorum. What's appropriate for the hot tub after midnight, isn't for Pastafari at seven.

Guests have fun flouting the silly rules, such as going to the main bar nude *before* midnight and streaking through the disco at a slow walk. Hedo allows nudity on the entire grounds after midnight.

The one real rule at Hedo: Don't harm yourself or anyone else. If you err on the side of outrageous, no problem; the atmosphere at Hedo is accepting and even forgiving.

Tales from the Naked City

After the wedding of a young couple, the minister said, "There is an old Jamaican custom. Whatever you do the first week of marriage doesn't count." Let me tell you this couple put it to test (they were swingers).

Later at night we were waiting in the Pastafari for them. At the time there was a strict dress code: no bare feet, no bare backs. My wife's dress was backless, so I pulled it up to cover her back (and then her ass showed). The newly married couple, dressed nicely, entered the restaurant to a warm applause, but they were asked to leave since they had no shoes on. They left and returned with shoes, took off all their clothes outside, and came in buck naked. Management went crazy until the couple picked up their feet and said, "But we got shoes on." Guests and staff broke out laughing.

—HedoHenry

Be courteous when taking pictures

The photography and video rules are about respect and courtesy. Privacy is difficult to maintain at Hedo, but not impossible.

Never take people's photo or use video without permission, even if they are only in the background. Just because someone looks interesting at Hedo, they are there for themselves, not for your photo opportunity. If you are taking pictures of naked people, be naked yourself.

Every guest identifiable in a picture or by name in this book has provided me with written permission for its use here and here alone. When everyone at Hedo respects everyone else, we all have a good time—just like in the real world.

The only times you don't have to ask permission is when people are on stage performing or receiving a prize, which includes the final display of the body painting on the nude beach. But that still means your pictures are only for personal consumption.

If you want to photograph the three gorgeous babes posing all over each other at the poolside for their husbands, ask permission of the ladies first. The pool is not a stage—even though performers might use it.

One man secretly made and sold a video (as porno) of people on the nude beach. He is reviled by all. Be careful whose video you pose for. The SuperClubs lawyers did find the person but didn't prosecute at the time because SuperClubs didn't want to give the videos further notoriety (thus more embarrassment to its guests) by suing the person, says Hedo general manager Kevin Levee.

Never put Hedo photographs on the Internet without express permission of the identifiable people. Just because someone lets you take the picture does not give you permission to use it outside your vacation photo album. This is true even if you bought the photograph from Color Negril, whose photographers take pictures of people in the dining area.

Guards often stop you from taking pictures on the nude beach—even if you are naked and your friends in the picture are not. That's because some guards are not well trained. The people being photographed should be firm in telling the guards that it's okay—and make sure no unwitting people are in the background. The guard eventually goes away.

If you see inappropriate photo taking and are not comfortable telling the person to stop, be firm with the guards to convince them to stop the offending guest.

Tipping is not allowed, but gifts are

Some guests believe you have to tip the bartenders for good service. This is not true. Service is as fast as you are nice. You have to be smiling, pleasant, and courteous to guarantee good service at Hedo, just like at most places in the real world.

The Hedo staff risks job loss if caught receiving a tip. To reward good service, be discreet. You can tell them quietly you'd like to give them a tip. The person will tell you how best to transfer it.

You may give the staff gifts, however. Put the gift in a cute shopping bag for them to take it home in. And if you leave the maid a gift, such as your creams, toys, or clothes, make sure you enclose a signed note with the items listed so she is not accused of theft.

Here are some items especially appreciated by Jamaicans:
T-shirts and caps with a sports imprint, especially NBA
Picture frames
Athletic shoes
Sunglasses
Children's clothes
Peanut butter
CDs and blank cassettes
Boom boxes
Paperback books
AA and D batteries
Aspirin and ibuprofen, antibiotics
Soap, shampoo, skin cream, makeup, and toiletries

Nails were popular after Hurricane Gilbert. If you have a Polaroid camera take a picture of someone and give it to him or her, or bring a picture framed on your next trip.

As you meet the staff, you learn what is special to them. Repeaters often come to Hedo with tons of luggage that is empty when they go home, except for coffee and Tia Maria.

Wedding bells ring

People marry in Jamaica because the ceremony is inexpensive and easy. A lot of people meet at Hedo and subsequently marry. A few people have even married in the nude, but fewer ministers permit it these days. The minister always wears a dark suit.

Tales from the Naked City

Every year our group decides in advance what costumes we will wear to goof on the guests and the staff. In August 1996 we decided to go as Nuns and Priests. We rented Father Guido Sarducci costumes for the guys, complete with long gowns with stiff white collars, big gold crosses, and padre hats. The Nuns had full-length old-style habits, gold crosses, and full head covers.

We waited until that night, and you had to see the faces of the guests when we arrive for dinner at one table. We were greeted with "Good evening, Father and Sister." The highlight of the week took place in Veronica's where two weddings were occurring in the game room at the same time. A bride saw us and asked us to bless their weddings. We made up a solemn blessing and had a good laugh.

A year later I shared a TimAir flight with two ministers. I thought the one minister looked familiar so I asked him if he did the weddings at Hedo. He nodded. I asked if he remembered the nuns and priests who did the wedding the year before. He said, "Shame on you, you are very bad people," and he smiled.

—Bob "Studman" Starz from New Jersey

Marina and George wed on the nude beach in November 1997 on their third trip to Hedo.

Let Hedo know one working week in advance about your desire to be married. The staff wedding coordinator prepares all details, such as arranging for the marriage license, the minister (who is a public official), the hand-tied floral bouquet, and the reception, which includes cake and champagne.

Jamaica requires certified copies of both parties' birth certificates, which must include the fathers' names. The occupations of the bride and groom must be stated. If either have been married before, Jamaica requires certification of final divorce papers or death certificates.

You also need to be in Jamaica at least 48 hours to marry. And you must stay at Hedo for at least three days for the hotel to foot the bill. Plan on waiting several weeks or months to receive the marriage certificate from Jamaican officials after you tie the knot.

SuperClubs offers free round-trip flights for the bride if she has her wedding in Jamaica at a SuperClubs resort. It's called the SuperBrides promotion. Call your travel agent for details.

One wedding on the fishhook jetty in 1997 enjoyed an au naturel flower girl. Joyce had painted Karen from neck to knees in acrylics with a full-length floral bouquet.

Get married right before sunset on the jetty or on the pier or under the trees on the nude beach. The bird aviary and gardens are often too warm. Sunset in late November is at 5:30 p.m.

Some brides wear real meringue-like dresses. Some wear slutwear. Others wear regular dresses. Half the grooms I've seen wear jackets. And a little under half the couples are barefoot.

The champagne and cake reception, held in the game room of Veronica's is usually short. At dinner the staff will decorate a congratulations table if you request it.

Tales from the Naked City

A Kansas football player and his girlfriend got married in the bar and fed each other cake from their genitals.

Hedo is physically safe, but lock up your goodies

People have willingly lost their virginity at Hedo, but the women have never lost the box it came in. Old joke.

Overall, Hedo is exceptionally safe. The hotel really looks out for you.

People have reported missing cameras, money, and jewelry from their rooms, but this is not a common occurrence. Theft on the beach only occurs if you leave something after dark. Most people leave their bags unattended on the beach all day, but don't leave cameras and sunglasses out for easy pickup (by sticky-fingered guests).

Lock all your valuables, plane tickets, passports, etc., in the safe located in the room closet. Keep the safe key with you at all times (or cleverly hidden in the room).

Thieves enter first-floor rooms more easily than second-floor rooms, but this is a rare problem because the guards are everywhere (even in the bushes, it seems) and watching guests closely.

I've never felt unsafe walking alone around the grounds of Hedo on the darkest of nights. Although I've heard stories of the rare rape, the odds of its occurrence, unless you go with a stranger who is rapist to a room, are tiny.

If someone comes to your door asking for a contribution, call the front desk to report it immediately, even if the person has official-looking papers. He or she is a thief.

If a Jamaican you don't know well asks you if you want to see the real Jamaica, don't go. You'll either see the real Jamaica and pay exorbitant sums along the way, or the ride could be dangerous.

Protect your health

Hedo has no strange incidence with disease that is peculiar to it except DIF (Dreaded Island Fever) that makes guests return to Hedo. Illness spreads rapidly through most vacation resorts because of the physical closeness of people. If one person has a cold, everyone gets a cold. Also, any beach vacation can make people sick because they are out of their routine and they're in the ocean, which has tons of weird viruses.

The nurse station keeps busy at Hedo. One year, the pestilence started with Towelhead's big toenail falling off from playing basketball with too-tight shoes. After that the pattern of rot spread: colds, stomach upset, diarrhea, ear infection (gonorrhea of the ear from aural sex, no doubt), and heart problems. But the ailments gave the guests something to talk about and they all lived.

Watch for foot injuries from glass and sea urchins. The island remedy for urchin needles is to pee on the affected area (ammonia in urine dissolves the needles), but no one has let me provide the cure no matter how persistently I offer.

A variety of ailments can befall you. Traveler's diarrhea is a biggie in Jamaica. Bring the Pepto, PepcidAC, and whatever else you might need.

The nurse station at Hedo is not well equipped for unusual emergencies, but paramedics and a doctor in Negril can come.

Although few people are vaccinated against hepatitis, getting vaccinated is not a bad idea because the disease is afflicting more and more people in the world and is easily transmitted. The hotel sprays often for mosquitoes so they are not of critical concern.

Whatever you aren't prepared for can cost you big money. In 1997, a sober friend fell off the sidewalk (She says I pushed her, but I'm still denying it.) and required a gazillion sutures in her knee—$400 U.S.—cash.

Book through a travel agent

Any travel agent can book a vacation to Hedo for you. Many travel agents specialize in Hedo and can sometimes give you a better rate because they book such huge quantities for the hotel.

Here are some travel agencies Hedo guests have recommended. This list is not complete or in any order, and I have no vested interest in or opinion of any of them. I book through the hotel, but that's not commonly allowed, so don't bother trying if you haven't done it before.

Lifestyles, Tours and Travel, California, 800-359-9942
www.playcouples.com

Go Classy Tours in Palm Harbor, Fla.
800-329-8145 or 800-329-8148; fax 813-781-1305
www.goclassy.com

A discount travel agency to the Caribbean: 800-405-4787

Global Tours, 918-250-6069

Moment's Notice, 718-234-6295

All-Inclusive Vacations, www.all-inclusive.com
909-824-2998; fax 909-824-2997

Ray@lighthousetravel.com

Funjet at www.funjet.com

Jeannie's Specialty Tours at tjvodnik@execpc.com
414-425-2582 (especially for Celebration of Body Arts)

How to get discounts and free days

Regulars tend to figure out a system for reducing the costs of their trips. By paying for 14 days in a calendar year, guests are eligible for three free days but need a letter from Hedo's general manager confirming that. You must have that letter for your travel agent. Just be pleasant but persistent to receive paperwork from the hotel.

SuperClubs, the owners of Hedonism II, also has what it calls a Sunshine Guarantee. If from daybreak to sunset the sun doesn't shine even once, you receive a voucher for one free day

on your next trip. Often you must pester the front desk a lot to receive this voucher. SuperClubs also has freebie deals if a hurricane hits.

Each Wednesday night Hedo hosts a cocktail party for repeat guests and gives a complimentary week to a person in the crowd who has made the most trips to Hedo but who hasn't won before. Travel agents and people who are enjoying complimentary trips can't participate. Sometimes people win at six trips, but mostly numbers in the lower teens win.

If you have a particular skill Hedo can use, you can work during your vacation and negotiate with the general manager for a discount.

Hedo is so desperate to increase the number of single women at the resort it offers women a discount. Four women booking together for two rooms pay only the cost of three—a 25% discount. Also, if three women are willing to be in a room together (third bed brought in), then only two have to pay—a 33% discount.

Beautiful people swarm to the media

Various magazines, television specials, and radio shows go to Hedo to report on it or use the resort as a backdrop. During the late spring and summer, the media are more prevalent at Hedo.

Swimwear Illustrated and *Penthouse* have held photo shoots. *Inside Edition* taped its programs at Hedo. Memphis Tennessee Rock 103 radio station broadcast its show from Hedo along with 170 Tennessee volunteers.

People who want to see and be seen book these media weeks. The number of beautiful people on the beaches increases exponentially during media weeks. So does the quantity of saline, silicone, and blond hair. The average age of the guests at Hedo goes down too. Thong suits are everywhere, ostensibly to maintain interesting tan lines for professional reasons.

A lot of wannabes try to make their debut during media weeks—porn stars and strippers abound. A strip club in Atlanta called Cheetah did its still photos for its annual calendar last May when Playboy's *Night Calls* was filming.

Wherever the *Night Calls* gals congregated for the camera they were spanking each other and screaming aloud. For the beach party they wore grass skirts, even though Hedo is in the Caribbean, not the South Pacific.

Hedo has a summertime calendar shoot too: A contest for "The Ultimate Men of Hedonism II" where hunks compete for a monthly designation.

Chapter 3

Nudes rule, Prudes drool

A friendly rivalry exists between the Nudes and the Prudes at Hedo—unless one group invades the beach space of the other. Then some people get ugly.

You know which group you belong to by where you spend your day: clothed on the prude beach or nude on the clothing-optional beach, which isn't really clothing-optional. When facing the water, the nude beach is right of the concrete pier that divides Hedo's long stretch of beach into two separate beaches.

The Prude designation has nothing to do with sexual mores. My observations show single Prudes mate slightly more than single Nudes do.

Tales from the Naked City

Two guys in a kayak wandered into the roped-off swimming area of the nude beach. They paddled into some people because they were too busy looking at naked bodies. I was sunning myself nearby on one of the deck floats so I slipped into the water, swam under the kayak, and tipped them over. Two other people swam over and depantsed the guys as they floundered. The guys had to walk nude up to the beach to retrieve their trunks. All the way up, they tried hiding their private parts. Their faces were as red as a Negril sunset—and not from sunburn either.

—Denny Pasternak, Omaha, Neb.

When Nudes invade the prude beach, the occasional person will get mad and ask the guards to tell the Nudes to go away. Mostly the Prudes just whip their cameras out. Nudes seldom are on the prude beach except when walking through it or otherwise torturing the Prudes with some game.

When Prudes invade the nude beach (walk on it clothed—an unfortunate, common activity), they are considered lurkers. The Nudes become agitated and react in various ways. Some yell mean things. Some are friendly and try to encourage disrobing. Some force a disrobing (rare). Some ignore the Prudes. Others sic the guards on them. Some give out a warrant:

Warrant for Arrest

Charges:

Having appeared on the Nude Beach wearing inappropriate textiles, you:

Stimulated and provoked puritanical thoughts and ideas, which have absolutely no redeeming social value.

And have demonstrated the perverse, antisocial personality disorder of voyeurism while clothed.

Determination:

You are guilty of insidious and Victorian thoughts.

Execution:

Fines and punishments shall be administered in the following prescribed manner:

Immediate expulsion from the nude beach.

Loss of all bar privileges for the next 10 minutes.

Eternal vilification by all as a Prude.

Notice:

This citation shall be null and void upon immediate removal of all offensive clothing and payment of a fine not to exceed two drinks of the arresting officer's choice.

Demographics of Hedo guests

Hedo has a cross section of normal and not-so-normal people. Both add to the atmosphere. Some say you'll never meet a better class (all low), as you will at Hedo.

Tales from the Naked City

One Tuesday night the disco bartenders served beer in plastic water cups, presumably to prevent broken glass and the injuries that can happen. Wine and other drinks were still served in glassware, though. When I asked why they were still using glass for these beverages, I was told "because the plastic was thought to be too tacky for a nightclub." I looked around to be sure that the woman with the nipple clamps next to me didn't have a plastic cup.

—Doug from Pennsylvania

Some people are predictable. People from California never stop telling you how it never rains at home and the sun is always out at home. Someone from Wisconsin always talks about the Packers and how cold it is at home.

"We are a motley crew of total idiots and drunken louts. Join our crusade! I take this opportunity to extend a well-used double-ended dildo to you to cement the lasting bond of total debauchery and complete lunacy that is central to our cause."

—Chris Carignan from Toronto

In the Hedo brochures, everyone is young and in perfect shape. This is a lie. The average age at Hedo is 35 to 55, but the range is 18 to 90+, with people in all stages of physical condition.

Don't worry about that age thang; it doesn't matter at Hedo—unless people start acting their age...be it low or high. No one is out of place at Hedo based on age. The wrong attitude puts you out of place.

Tales from the Naked City

I rush up to Jim to give him a big bare hug...when I realize he is wrapped in a towel. "This is a nude pool," I laughingly remind him. As I remove his towel, I realize that I have been set up. "Do you know what time it is, young lady?" he asks. Jim has strategically placed a watch around his privates. An astute lady in the pool calls over, "Hey! Is that one of those watches that takes a licking and keeps on ticking?"

—Nancy Griffin

Hard bodies generally stay on the prude side. The prude pool can look like a "Spring Break" movie set with young people posturing and gawking at each other from behind copious numbers of plastic drink glasses.

A typical guest demographic, though, is: white, American married man, age 44, with similar-age first- or second-marriage wife, both with 20 extra pounds and upper-middle class living style in the mid-Atlantic with two kids. They go to Hedo to pep up their sex life, chat all day with old and new friends, and take a relaxing vacation.

"Lots of people don't sleep around but still want to be wicked. Since it's with their spouse there is no recrimination, no cheating, and we get a little fantasy in our lives after being married for a long time. Hedo is a great place to recharge a marriage. There are plenty of 'sleep arounds' who wouldn't be caught dead at Hedo."

—RMincold

Jim from Milwaukee and Chris from Chicago play at the Turtle's garden party.

About 50% of the guests at any time are couples. Couples come to Hedo because other resorts are quiet after 10 p.m., and, as Hedo general manager Kevin Levee says, "They can get silly and put on a toga."

Sure, you are going to find the young porn star with her middle-age husband-manager. You'll also see the 25-year-old short, stocky, single guy from New Jersey on his first trip away from the East Coast and the newly divorced 47-year-old, paunchy, bald guy on the make with the 23-year-old babes. Adonis and Barbie are there too. All types go to Hedo.

Joe from Pennsylvania, using someone's leftover "Manogram" costume from the Halloween party, ensures the women have healthy glands.

Why be naked?

Many Hedo guests gain or have a fascination with nudity. Comfort is the key word with nudity.

Imagine rolling out of bed naked. Wipe the sleep from your eyes (euphemism for perform morning bathroom rituals) and walk out your room. The sun warms your skin all over and the soft, humid breeze tickles.

Greet another naked friend, and make your way to the nude beach, towel in hand. Sit naked on your towel, sip coffee with friends, and watch and listen to the gentle ocean waves. Sure, you could do this with clothes on (after you take the time to choose them and put them on), but you won't feel as fresh, and as surprisingly comfortable, as you would naked in the Tropics.

> "We have found it difficult to explain to most people about the trip because they cannot get past the nude beach. How do you describe the lifestyle of acceptance and freedom, the fun, the friendships, and the like? It becomes incredibly frustrating to attempt to describe it all when most people can't get past the 'you were on a nude beach?' I am beginning to understand why some people tell their friends they go next door to Grand Lido to avoid the hassle of trying to explain."
> —Paul Kuhn from Chicago, age 32

Think in terms of sunlight warming your genitals and soft breezes through your pubic hair—if you have it.

Think in terms of no serious burn lines at the edge of your swimsuit.

Think about the smooth roundness of your fat without the indent of a swimsuit's elastic emphasizing its mush.

You avoid crotch-rot because a birthday suit dries faster than a textile one. You don't have to pack multitudes of suits.

Boobs float too, giving them nonsurgical improvement in the sea or pool. And under water, the penis can look bigger because of refraction.

And most important: brown fat looks better than white fat.

But no one is looking at your fat because they're all looking at your private parts. Just kidding. Wear dark sunglasses to increase your viewing pleasure.

Hedonism cannot sustain its market if it were totally nude, general manager Kevin Levee says. "A lot of our guests don't know the hotel has a nude beach when they are arrive and start out on the prude beach. Many people experience nudity for the first time at Hedonism II," he says.

"On our first trip to Hedo we didn't know much about the place and were hotel hopping around Jamaica. We arrived late at night and went right to our room and crashed since we had been traveling for 16 hours.

The next day we opened the curtains to see where we were. Everyone was nude on the beach. My wife didn't believe me when I told her and dashed to the window to see for herself. Her jaw dropped and said no way was she going nude in public. She started yelling at me for taking her to a place like this and wondered what people would think. She was worried someone would see her and I said, 'So what? They will be nude too.'

We dressed for breakfast and opened the door and ran into our neighbors. They were nude and greeted us warmly. We were embarrassed to be talking to nude people and did not want to stare. They noticed we were uptight and asked if this was our first time to Hedonism II. My wife replied, 'First and last time.'

That was 12 trips and 12 years ago."

—George McLean

Nudity concerns pass quickly

Most people are pleasantly flawed. Modesty passes. You may end up in a discussion about your scars. Two surgeons might discuss breast implant surgery by casually evaluating all the jobs on the beach.

Some women proudly belong to the Itty Bitty Titty Club. Others are part of the Plastic Surgery Showcase—Bars and scars and lifts and tucks, all-inclusive for just a few bucks. One woman with a double mastectomy came to the beach with small implants and nipples tattooed on, and she looked lovely.

Tales from the Naked City

An older married Californian at Hedo with his young blond tootsie was staring at a plain, dark-haired woman walking the beach. "I like her; she's cute," he said. I asked why. "It's that overbite," he replied. "We don't have those in California."

Nudity is a great equalizer. Personality lies underneath skin—not on top of it. People are wrapped up in conversation and often pay no attention to the fact they are naked. That's probably why the nude beach has more socializing going on than the prude beach.

"The nudity bothered me in the beginning—for about a day. It is really the most natural thing to do, and *the* thing to do if you really want to enjoy the Hedo experience.

Besides, you have more fun because the people on the nude beach are friendly and talkative and really don't judge. They are just out for a good time."

—Sue from Chicago

Nudity is sensuous, but it's not always sexual. Erections are uncommon because the inspiration isn't there. Most men find women more sexually exciting at dinner when parts are covered in interesting ways. Mystery is sexy.

The first nude experience takes courage for some, who always laugh about it later. Others claim "No way is naked for me," and after five minutes on the beach they're flinging off clothes, leaving their husbands in happy amazement.

Getting naked isn't always easy because of social training. Hedo is training ground for new awareness.

"When we first went to Hedo, I was extremely prudish. I wouldn't even walk over to the nude beach for two days; even then I felt uncomfortable. By midweek I decided, what the hell, I'll take off my top—a big step for me. By Saturday, I said to myself, I'll never see these people again, so I went ahead and bared it all.

During that year after going, we didn't stop talking about Hedo and about how much fun it was. We actually recruited friends to come back with us, which was great.

When we arrived at Hedo for our second trip, I couldn't get on the nude beach fast enough. I was hooked by the third trip and ready to take my clothes off on the bus.

Going there is an experience a lot of people don't understand. They think all that goes on there are wild orgies and sex on the beach. I disagree. We have had a lot of great times there; we've been 16 times and can't wait to go again in October."

—Lo from New Hampshire, age 40

Don't ever fool yourself into thinking you'll not see these people again so anything you do is okay. You will see them again—at Hedo.

Beach etiquette and dynamics

I can't tell you much about the prude beach—haven't sat there in more than 10 years. The prude beach sand is only slight less gritty and hard-packed than the sand on the nude beach. People seem to stay in small groups of two or three and occasionally talk to others. Most socializing appears to occur at the bar or on the adjacent volleyball court. Actually the beach is pretty bare a lot of the time; I'm not sure where the Prudes are.

The nude beach is a cocktail party with lots of naked people lounging about and chatting. Naked people in the water, naked people standing at the new Delroy's Naked Bum Beach Bar, even naked people playing bocci ball. Every day resembles the premise of the movie "Ground Hog's Day": same routine with slight variation determined by you.

The nude beach engenders camaraderie. Maybe that's because you can't hide your hide. Can't lick 'em, may as well join 'em.

"For people wanting to relax, the sand gravity at Hedo is the strongest of any place in the Caribbean."
—Denny Pasternak from Omaha, Neb.

On the nude beach, however, everyone is jockeying for new positions since the building of the new nude pool and bar complex at the end of the nude beach in October 1996. The beach focus has changed. The action has moved from the middle of the beach (where the old Delroy's bar still stands as a massage shack) to the end of the beach. With all the action at the far end of the beach, fewer Prudes walk through—a pleasant side benefit.

The dynamics have changed though. Where once people could see each other because they were on the shore or in the ocean, now the Nudes are Pool people or Rafting people and they can't see each other. Some are definitely one way or the other; some switch off depending on time of day. Being neither provides exercise and gives you lots of daily occupation, walking back and forth between beach and pool. The problem with being one or the other is that you miss interesting activities because you can't quite observe one from the other as in the old days with only beach-to-sea activities to view.

People still float, but the huge raft flotillas of yesterday (like shipwrecked crew hanging onto one another) is not as prevalent. Water shoes are a good idea in the ocean because of the abundance of rocks and sea urchins.

On hot, steamy days the pool is overrun pleasantly and becomes quite the chat hole. Cooler days, it's empty. Some groups even hang by the hot tub all day.

People often pile chair pads and rafts on top of the loudspeakers sticking up from the sand to muffle them. Old beach favorites are seldom played, such as: "Candy Licker," "Don't Want No Short Dicked Man," and "Strokin'." All the music is now on compact disc instead of Delroy's infamous tapes.

The jetty, or fishhook, catches the morning sun before the rest of the nude beach.

Mornings are blissfully quiet until 10 a.m. when the beach bar opens and the music starts. For serenity, hang by Delroy's old bar where it's quiet. The old bar has working taps for water, soda, and (usually) beer that often flows after all the bars have closed at 5 a.m. if you need a fix before 10 a.m.

Many people arrive on the beach after 10:30 a.m. Early risers are hard-core tanners and water-sport aficionados.

Local artisans carve tree stumps on the beach or in the garden with your name, if you like. One guest paid $20 and a couple packs of cigarettes, for his and her names in a large heart. Some trees have interesting extensions carved into them that people stop to speculate about or hang underpants on.

The cool-water Jacuzzi (one of the four water focuses of the nude pool complex) has some jets with a force of about seven knots. But one jet is nice, according to one female guest who once dragged the beach chair into the cool-water Jacuzzi to lay back on as she threw her legs wide over the concrete edge of the pool for effect.

The foot-deep misting pool next to the cool-water Jacuzzi offers a grotto fronted by a waterfall. Called the fornicatorium or BJ Cave by some, it provides a venue for cave-stuffing parties (sometimes of 45 people or more), which can become a naughty event within.

Hedo even provides a bidet (fountain) outside the fornicatorium. Few women realize it's one of Hedo's finest additions. Ladies, remember to bring a gentleman to lean on, your legs become quite weak.

How to apply sunscreen

The sun is intense so bring sunscreen. For a two-week trip I take two bottles of two different SPFs and stay under the trees. A lot of people wear hats or visors too.

If you plan on exposing parts of your body not usually exposed to the sun, apply a high-SPF sunscreen there too.

Many people opt for the electric tan before coming to Hedo, as the white circles over their tailbones attest.

Remember to apply sunscreen to the boy parts—or get the wrinkles out—because of the cursed zebra dick disease that can occur with too much sun. Opt for a clear lotion because the white stuff draws verbal barbs.

Most people will be happy to do your back. If you are male, only good female friends or wives will put sunscreen on your butt.

And, men, don't ask the same person everyday unless you are sleeping with her. Don't go looking for a particular woman to put it on your back unless you already have an excellent relationship with her otherwise you are painfully obvious. If she doesn't want you in any way, someone will be unhappy about the whole ordeal.

Women, on the other hand, have different rules. We can preen and pose and bend over for easy access to our backs for the application of sun screen. (Oh look, I must pick up something from the sand again—and again.) God, I love sunscreen. Just make sure you are not SPF incompatible with whoever does the rubbing.

Be careful when combining the use of sunscreen, booze, and the large fiberglass platform rafts just off shore. By applying enough tanning oil and Bloody Marys, you can slide all the way across and off those suckers on a naked butt.

The most important part of getting an even tan is remembering to rotisserate: turn over sometime.

Tales from the Naked City

This is my first time on a nude beach, so give me some time. *Said by Greg on his first day at Hedo.*

Yes, let's all walk down to Sandals wearing only shaving cream bathing suits. *Said by Greg on his third day at Hedo.*

People practice for the best tan contest all day long. Instruction is also available from guests.

Beach chairs are aplenty; pads are more rare

Toweltoria instinct says that if you put a towel or inflatable raft on a beach chair at 8 a.m., the chair and position markers will be available at 4 p.m. when you actually want to use them.

If you touch someone's marked chair, your good name is besmirched.

Make sure to use a cushion on the beach chairs with slats or you will experience bum bands. Only periodically are cushions abundant, so bring an inflatable raft for flotillas and chair padding. Oftentimes old rafts are available, though, too.

If you prefer to sit upright rather than lounge, grab a plastic chair from just outside the dining area after breakfast and walk it to the beach.

Beware of falling asleep on the beach. HedoHenry reports that a friend fell asleep on the beach, at which point he was covered with shaving cream and sprinkles, minus his pubic hair, and had around 50 of the quietest naked people around him when he finally woke up.

Tales from the Naked City

Remember not to sit too close to the end of the beach chairs. Jim and Linda almost simultaneously sat down on the edges of their adjoining chairs and naturally toppled down into the sand as the other end shot into the air. But, much to their credit, they did not spill a drop of their drinks.

Bring your own raft

The most popular outdoor activity on the nude beach is floating on inflatable rafts in the calm of the water. Watch for the kamikaze diver, Pete the penguin, I mean pelican, and his fertilization.

Tales from the Naked City

"How early do you have to get up to get one of those rafts?" *Said by a first-timer who didn't know the program.*

Tales from the Naked City

A beautiful naked woman was spread eagle sunning her parts on a big raft. Passing boats from Sandals would come close to take a look. She'd then pick up the high-powered water gun hidden beneath her towel and blast 'em one.

Buy a $2 raft from K-Mart. Take it to the dive shop on the beach where the staff inflates it from a scuba tank. Bring a large waterproof marker and write your name or nickname on one end and write "please use after 'date.'" Leave it on the beach for others to enjoy when you depart. An October raft was still in good shape in February when mutual friends found it.

Many left-behind rafts litter the beach, but you don't know if they are unclaimed until they don't move for a day or two. Take rafts to your room to guarantee keeping them all week.

Tales from the Naked City

One year I found a blow-up sheep on my beach chair with my nickname "Studman" on it. Since I go to Hedo single, the gang thought I needed a companion. We called her Baabette. Naturally, we had the round of jokes such as, "What did Baabette say when you asked for sex? Naaa. Was the sex good? Yaaah. Our songs were "Only Ewe" and "I've Got Ewe Under My Skin."

About midweek I brought Baabette to breakfast. I left her alone five minutes and she was kidnapped. The ransom note demanded $1 million or lamb chops would be served that night. We started a fund-raiser to save Baabette. The next morning I left a fake check for the ransom, and by noon I found her in the middle of the stage at lunchtime spin. I tried to have her checked for AIDS, but the nurse said the test would deflate her ego.

—Bob "Studman" Starz from New Jersey

People on the prude beach tend to sit in the beach chairs, likely because they are first-timers and didn't know to bring a raft. If you lose your raft, check the prude beach for it. Stealing rafts back from a Hedo first-timer is always an adventure and gives you something to gripe about.

If you bring an inflatable raft with holes that can hold drink cups, you will be popular and make bars runs easier. Just ask Delroy for a raft full, which is 18 drinks.

People also bring inflatables of unusual shapes—musical instruments, islands with palm trees, Puff the dragon, and dolls and sheep—with or without working orifices.

Stock up on beach towels

Many locations have beach towels, but not all are stocked all the time. Make it a habit to pick up some towels when you see them, since fresh ones are harder to find later in the day. People often stash 147 towels in their closets for emergencies.

Some people prefer to bring beach towels from home, but you don't need to.

If you lug a wet towel back to your room and leave it in a heap on the floor, the maid likely will fold it and put it in the corner for you to trade in later. Often the staff requires you to return a towel to get another one.

One guest found the mother lode of towels: take the sidewalk from the hot tub to the bathrooms. Go behind the building and in the door. At night lots of clean towels are stashed in there (also you'll find the controls to the temperature to the hot tub, which is handy because sometimes it is too hot and sometimes too cold).

Tales from the Naked City

She fell off the beach. *Said by Barbara when someone asked her why Lori Beth was wearing a bandage on her wrist.*

The infamous Hot tub is for all comers

Heliomigration to the hot tub (the last of four water pools in the nude pool complex) occurs after sunset or about 6 p.m. in the summer. Reports indicate 355 people once sprayed champagne all over one other while standing in the huge, clover-shaped tub.

Two buttons near the edge of the hot tub activate the tub jets. Many a novice has sat on them, thus shutting off the bubbles. The newbie must then bring everyone a fresh drink.

Seeing action in the hot tub is not a predictable event. And it's not the norm at cocktail hour when the tub is crowded with chatterers. Sometimes it's dead at midnight. Tuesday's PJ party brings out a good crowd after 1 a.m., though.

Tales from the Naked City

I was walking down the past to the hot tub with a lady, and she inquired about the palm trees with all the names on them. I turned and bowed my head and told her they were for all the couples who died having sex in the hot tub. She believed me, and the next day had her friends there all saying prayers for the dead. I was afraid to tell her the truth after that because she did have a religious experience: The night before she kept saying "Oh God, oh God."

—Bob "Studman" Starz from New Jersey

Guests joke about getting athlete's vagina from sitting on the side of the pool, as they dangle their feet. People have picked up an itchy skin rash in the hot tub, but it's not a common occurrence. The sand fleas on the beach at sunset are more insidious.

The tub water is heavily treated, but some don't go in on principle. Others don't go in because they don't want the chemicals to fade their tan. Hedo has an annoying way of chemically treating the pool and hot tub at dinnertime, and it is often closed from 8 p.m. to 10 p.m.

Much of the orgoslag what you find floating in the hot tub is spilled banana drinks, suntan oil, and beach crud. The squeamish object when the semen content in the hot tub gets over 33%. Just kidding.

Don't miss the green flash at sunset

Everyone hopes to see the green flash at sunset, but few people do. The green flash can exist. It is a thin green band visible for a split second just above the top edge of the sun as it sinks below the horizon. Sometimes the flash is violet or blue or turns from green to blue. To see the green flash, you need a clear horizon and a haze-free sky.

Atmospheric refraction causes the green flash. Air bends sunlight and splits it into a rainbow of colors. Refraction causes the sun to be surrounded by ghost images, with a violet-blue-green shadow above and a red-orange-yellow one below. This refraction is greatest at sunrise and sunset, when the sunlight is so reduced that the ghost images don't wash out. The red ghost can't be seen because it is below the horizon, and the atmosphere absorbs the orange and yellow. The blue and violet ones scatter, leaving the green one.

If you attend sunsets regularly, you will see a green flash in your lifetime. But remember to leave the beach right after sunset, because the sand fleas (nasty biting insects that no one has actually ever seen) come out when the sand temperature cools.

Tales from the Naked City

When I get home I'm going to sit around the house wearing nothing but glitter and drinking out of plastic cups. *Said by Steve as he boarded the bus to return home.*

Bad things about Hedo

Trying to remember someone's name from a previous trip who seems to think you are best of friends

Listening to repetitious techno-rap music in the disco

Having to put underpants on when you leave the hotel

Arriving late to dinner and finding you missed a tasty entree because supplies ran low

Dealing with overzealous guards

Covering your ears because some coordinators don't know how to use a microphone well

Finding that little piece of paper (eviction notice) under your door that says you must go home

Finding out it's Delroy's vacation week

Attending the repeat-offender's party when lobster is unavailable and the tenderloin just ran out

After your first trip, realizing you should have been coming here years before

Ruining your beach vacation plans forever because you don't want to go anywhere else

Lingering through The Last Day at Hedo

Taking the long bus ride in either direction

Getting a prude room when you booked a nude room

Having to spend your first night at the Point Village next door when Hedo is overbooked

"I remember once back in 1989 or 1990, I had a crummy time at Hedo. My memory is a bit hazy, but I think it was between 10:00 and 10:15 on a Tuesday morning, and I was hung over, and I swore I would never, ever, ever drink another drop of alcohol in my life, but then 10:15 rolled around, and someone offered me one of Delroy's mucho spicy Bloody Marys, and that was the end of that."

—Parfumier (formerly on AOL)

Lurking, jerking single guys

Hedo has its many types: the swingers, the old nudists, the spunky people, the bimbos, and the group everyone loves to hate: The Residudes. These are single men who hang around hoping to meet desperate women.

Residudes go by many names. At Hedo some call the old ones Wallies. These guys are often naked, but they stare and seldom speak. Some people feel creepy around them, but Wallies are harmless and usually painfully shy or perverted beyond words.

Tales from the Naked City

Then there was this really old guy...every time a couple embraced in the hot tub he'd be next to them like a shot—in nanoseconds he was in their lap. He just wanted to watch and the old eyes just weren't what they used to be. One rainy afternoon five couples arranged themselves in the middle and in each of the four clover leaves of the hot tub, and on my signal one of the couples (usually the one farthest from this guy) would stage an episode. The guy would bolt to the active couple then they'd stop, and I'd signal another couple to start. He swam about five miles in the hot tub that afternoon.

—Chris Everett, a.k.a. Hedoman,
from Pennsylvania, age 45

The young Residudes are frequently called Vinnies. On the East Coast, Vinnie is a derogatory term for Italian-Americans. At Hedo, though, Vinnie is a generic name for inconsiderate and inappropriate youth.

Some women go by the nickname "beach slut," and no one thinks any less of them, though society labels sluts as bad. Hedonism II flavors words differently.

Tales from the Naked City

Some guy at Hedo with a heavy New Jersey accent called to me from upstairs and said he wanted me to come up—no doubt he liked my dress. I said I couldn't because I hurt my foot. He proceeded to hop on one foot to show me how I could come upstairs. Now mind you, he's short, swarthy, tattooed, drunk and naked, with parts flopping. I walked away saying "you've offered me no reason to come up." His offering—with genuine earnest: "I've got a prick you could suck on." As I continued to walk away, I said, "I don't need to floss my teeth right now."

Vinnies are cliché at Hedo, but seldom a real problem. I like Vinnies—as pets. They are always true to form. They provide a topic of laughter. Embarrassing them is a fun, tactical trick...you draw them in carefully then slam them to the ground using a smile on your face and words that are beyond their vocabulary range: "Oh my, you are so beguiling, I could just lapidate you!" The Vinnie straightens up and looks smug, not knowing that lapidate means to throw stones.

Tales from the Naked City

A young man was taking the boat to the Island Picnic. He asked a staff member, "This water, does it go all the way around the island?"

You can also make Vinnies into raft slaves to fetch your drinks. Never tell them about the sea urchins, though, and then watch them limp away as they try to act cool. Hedo needs its clowns.

Tales from the Naked City

Vinnies can be a lot of fun. The prude hot tub was full of them when we were all playing Fuzzy Duck, a drinking game. My wife excused herself to go to the bathroom. As she was getting back in the hot tub, her top fell off. One Vinnie said, "God, I love Hedo!"

I saw one of the Vinnies the next day. He told me "When I woke up this morning, I was still drunk. It was so cool!" That line pretty much set the stage for the whole week.

—Mike from Naperville, Ill., age 37

Vinnies consider everyone on the nude beach a bunch of old people trying to party, but they sure seem to want to be on the nude beach a lot. Vinnies are often one-shot guests and seldom seen at Hedo a second time.

Tales from the Naked City

I'm checking into the hotel. A Vinnie is checking in beside me. I hear the accent and comment, "I bet you're from New York." He says, "Yeah, how jew guess?" I said, "People usually sound like where they're from. Can you guess where I'm from?" He couldn't. I told him Chicago. He responded, "I once dated a girl from Arizona."

Vinnies expect to have horny, nude women flung at their feet. When this doesn't happen, they blame the resort and start to drink more heavily in larger groups of fellow Vinnies.

Vinnies walk on the nude beach in huge shorts that cover waist to knee. Packs of clothed Vinnies believe they should be able to cruise the nude beach and not be bothered. Their rationale? "I paid the same money as youse did."

Tales from the Naked City

A single, older-than-40 man of distinctly Italian descent was standing around naked, as is just, waiting for Robert to take his sandwich order. A Vinnie, wearing the obligatory jams, asked him, "Do you speak English?" The older man shrugged his shoulders as though he didn't understand. The Vinnie retorted, "Hey, you got a small dick." Smiling, the older man, says, "Yeah, but your wife likes it."

The proper comment to Vinnies visiting the nude beach is "Nice textiles," roll your eyes, and smirk. Or women can use "God, those shorts are cute! Can I wear them?" and then convince them to disrobe. Some do.

Women can also con Vinnies into nakedness by stopping a pack of them as they walk the nude beach and starting a "best knees" contest and line them up for judging. Next move to butts, then naked butts, and by then, on request, some Vinnies actually do penises too.

Vinnies do drop trou in the hot tub after cover of darkness in their desperate plight to get what they came to Hedo for.

Male Vinnies tend to all look the same:

> Black high-top tennis shoes with no socks
> Long baggy shorts that extend below the knees
> Sleeveless shirts at dinner
> Heavy gold neck chains and pinkie ring
> Greased short hair
> Short, tattooed, stocky, yet muscular

Girls can be Vinnies too. They have discernible voices and their ability to intake alcohol is matched by their need to steal the microphone in the piano bar and do a kick dance to "New York, New York" fully clothed on the piano.

Tips to avoid being labeled a Vinnie

Don't hang out in the gym area with your gut hanging out, grunting while trying to lift more weight than you have since high school, thinking you impress women.

Do not hang out at the nude hot tub with clothes on.

Do not hang out at the nude beach with clothes on.

Don't bring glass to the nude pool and beach area.

Do not attempt to take the entire seafood tray at dinner; the food only gets cold while you wait for your 10th beer at the bar. And no, Hedo doesn't carry MGD.

Do not attempt to wear all your gold jewelry in the pool or ocean. It will weigh you down, especially after those five trips to the lunch buffet.

Do not hog the bar trying to explain a drink made in some Brooklyn bar by some guy named Chico, which you got trashed on after your cousin Bobby's wedding, usually all included in the description of said drink.

Stop the group vomiting sessions by 3 a.m.

Don't laugh when nothing is funny.

Don't grab or continuously ogle women.

Do not ask somebody's wife if she wants to get laid. Chances are she does, but not by you, and especially not your four drooling friends that have just eaten all the bar pretzels in Veronica's. (All tips found on AOL Hedo message board.)

Vinnie

V arious
I ndividuals,
N ot
N ude,
I nvading
E njoyment of the nude beach.

— Steve from Knoxville, Tenn., married, age 52

A treatise on Vinnies

By Doug from Pennsylvania

Vinnies are creatures not unlike locusts. Predictable and unavoidable. They swarm constantly to Jamaica (more often when Florida is full) and usually during spring break time for colleges. They are young, loud, impatient, and rude. Their language is colorfully laced with "F" words and the primitive ability to yell at Jamaicans and demand service. This is usually accompanied by banging of fists on the bar.

The Vinnie is seldom without its natural coat—muscle tops, shorts, and sneakers. Gold jewelry adorns the males. Voyeurism is their top hobby—losing themselves on the nude beach for hours at a time.

After nightfall, the obnoxious behavior of the Vinnies increases. They create a theater-like atmosphere at the nude hot tub, waiting for just the right time to say something rude to a women (or her boyfriend or husband) or generally behave in childlike wonderment of adult human sexuality. The Vinnie believes all women are polygamous and therefore a trophy for their inflated egos.

The chances of encountering one alone is rare—they travel in packs. Beer and flaming shots are their staple. Most suffer from AIDS (All-Inclusive-Disease Syndrome): they figure since they've paid for it, they're going to eat it and drink it. They often pass out in it. Their attempts at mating become increasingly humorous or annoying as the week progresses. Avoid at all costs.

Anthropological studies on the Vinnie

By Parfumier (formerly on AOL)

Vinnie (*Vinnibus bigbellibus*), of the genus Assholae, is a particular variant of the Northeastern Male (*Guyus ordinarius*). Prevalent in the New York and New Jersey area of the Northeastern United States, the Vinnie exhibits marked traits of self-delusion, particularly in its infrequent dealings with female members of related species.

The Vinnie is frequently characterized by his favorite vocalization: "Yo," as in "Yo, Vinnie."

Vinnies tend to travel in small packs of like individuals, since others like them are generally the only ones who will tolerate their company and their endless exaggerated stories of sexual conquest and alcohol overconsumption.

Despite their self-styled sexual reputations, they are rarely seen in the company of a member of the opposite sex, and their mating habits are still largely unknown. Curiously, there appears to be little interest in the study of this area of their behavior, possibly due to the extremely rare incidence of a Vinnie "getting lucky."

Given their resultant, well-documented tendency toward autostimulatory practices, some have suggested that they reproduce asexually, through some form of spontaneous mitosis, or similar cloning mechanism. This would be consistent with the diminutive, almost vestigial nature of their sexual/reproductive organs. We have been able to confirm, through necropsies performed on several drowned examples, that there is considerable hair growth on the palms of the hands.

During certain periods of the year, usually March, large numbers of them flock to all-inclusive resorts on the Caribbean island of Jamaica, where they congregate in larger pods, usually on beaches and around beer bars. These gatherings, reminiscent in some ways of the enormous gatherings of bull elephant seals at Alaskan rookeries, appear to be mock mating rituals, which we understand only superficially. We reach this conclusion due to the almost total absence of females of related species.

Surprisingly, under the circumstances, homosexual behavior is rare, although elaborate backslapping, arm-punching, high-fiving, and similar ritualistic homoerotic behavior is common. However, the presence of even a single female at such gatherings invariably provokes the characteristic call of "Yo, baby! Check it out! Wanna gimme some?" These calls are frequently accompanied by codified gestures, the meanings of which we do not yet fully understand, involving finger patterns and repetitive digital thrusting motions.

One observer has suggested that these gestures may, in fact, be a form of rehearsal for mating behavior once the Vinnie reaches sexual maturity. However, countervailing opinion holds that as no Vinnie has ever been observed reaching reproductive maturity, the rehearsal hypothesis remains unproven.

Small numbers of Vinnies have been observed gathering surreptitiously near the bathing places of mixed male and female couples, where they appear to watch mating behavior covertly, with obsessive fascination. Indeed, some Vinnies have been known to sit in hot water, motionless for hours, save for the slow turning of the head in the direction of mating couples, until their skin becomes soft and puckered, and through heat-induced vasodilatation, blood flow to the smallish brain is impaired. At such times, the Vinnie, in a lemming-like self-destructive impulse, slides slowly under the water to drown. Oddly, no one notices.

The Vinnie's eating habits are unremarkable, consisting mainly of high-fat, high-calorie foods that assist in providing a blubber layer insulating them against the worst effects of Northeastern winters. Their preferred source of carbohydrates appears to be beer, which they can be seen consuming until either the beer runs out or the Vinnie collapses in a pool of his own vomit. The implications of this behavior are unclear, although strict rules of Darwinian selection suggest that those members of the species unable to drink and remain conscious will be rejected from the pack and left to wander aimlessly and alone, eventually to drown themselves (see above).

Certain other common traits include abundant gold chains, baseball caps worn backward; baggy athletic shorts from a variety of well-known academic institutions, which, invariably, the Vinnie has not attended; and tight tank tops that emphasize their unusually large bellies and beefy shoulders tufted with hair (see also "Orang-Utang"). They are also occasionally seen affecting the style of wearing high-top athletic shoes with the laces undone, although the question has frequently been posed among researchers as to what real use the Vinnie would have for athletic apparel. Even ritualistic use appears unlikely, since the shoes, when worn, are worn for days at a time, and are seldom removed.

We have been unable to determine if the apparel described above has some significant ceremonial component, as it appears to be worn under any circumstances, including feeding, beer-drinking, and during autostimulatory excursions to the mixed couples' bathing areas.

Under the aegis of the endangered species act, active consideration is being given by the Wildlife Service to a concerted eradication program, although funding may be hard to allocate under present budgetary constraints.

Repeaters are surprisingly organized

Over the years many people have actually organized themselves into groups because they kept seeing the same people at Hedo each time they went. Some groups have names, some even send out newsletters and have dues. These dues cover the cost of mailings and the making and bringing of beach toys and paraphernalia.

Groups include the Tub Time Slushers, Golden Nuggets, Flamingos, Club Rub, Tilley Bares, and Eric's The Boston Bad Boy and Company, who once held a 32-person squirt gun fight during dinner. Whenever repeaters are at Hedo, they seem to want to form a group. Only a few occasionally make outsiders feel unwelcome, but none do all the time. Other well-known groups include:

Celebration of Body Art. This is a late September gathering of people decorated with tattoos and piercings. They go to Hedo at other times too.

Bubbly Bares. Numbering about 200, 40 to 60 usually show over Halloween/Anniversary and toward the beginning of March. They celebrated their 15th anniversary in February 1998. They are mostly couples, but do have some singles. They require dues and sponsorship to join. They are not a swing group, just old friends, who often travel to other destinations together now too. Their Thursday Champagne parties are luscious. And their men are cute in drag on Bimbo night.

Tales from the Naked City

Jimbo and his pranksters strike again: At the 15th Anniversary party week, the general manager's Honda somehow ended up in the main hallway between the front desk and the dining area. Doors locked, no keys, and a note inside "WIN THIS CAR! Collect 30,000 tokens and it's yours." The car stayed there all week.

Jimbo and his men in black masterminded one of his ultimate pranks: moving everything from the chair to the pictures on the wall in the general manager's office to the beach.

Pinpals. These friends return over Veteran's Day each year. Their name comes from a hot tub experience. A guard asked, with a distinct Jamaican accent, "Do you have a pin, mon?" The naked hot tubbers finally figured out that he wanted a pen, not a pin. No one in the hot tub had one. How strange. But the name stuck.

Butt Crack Tour. These fun-loving folk arrive about the third week in April. Poopsie and Rev JimBob Feelgood lead the gang on butt crack tours armed with whistles and large inflatables of men's private parts (in honor of the Macy Day parade) to adjoining hotels, especially Sandals, where they parade about and touch wood to wood (the wood fence at the end of Sandals' property).

Lifestyles. Married or those in committed relationships who share a desire for socio-sexual fun with other like-minded people sometimes call themselves Lifestylers. They attend Hedo during the last three weeks of January and usually over

Independence Day. Hedo always has its share of couples who swing every week though.

On the Edge. This group of friends commonly appears over Valentine's Day. Now the edge of the property is where the action is, so their fringeness is suddenly mainstream.

White Hats. A group of lecherous friends, under 20 in total, who show up the third week of February; some of the men wear White Hats to play nude beach patrol against evil.

Turtles. Once with members in the hundreds, this group is starting to dwindle. Captain Bob leads them. They arrive over Halloween/Anniversary and mid-February and enjoy Mardi Gras parades and garden parties.

The Hedo Turtles are an extension of a worldwide organization of service people dating back to WWII. Being a Turtle was a way of getting a conversation going in a strange bar or port. You'd ask "Are you a Turtle?" If they are and didn't reply with "You bet your sweet ass I am," they owed you a drink. If they had never heard of Turtles, the conversation started easily. Since any Turtle's prized possession is his donkey (ass), he is willing to bet his sweet ass in acknowledging he is a Turtle.

You become a Turtle by answering three simple questions that prove your innocence. One question is: What is hard and round and sticks out of a man's pajama's so far you can hang a hat on it? The answer is his head. Another Turtle tradition at Hedo is Dalmatian night when they dress as spotted dogs.

Biff's Bunch. With 120 members or so, this group meets at the end of April or beginning of May. Their motto Excess in Moderation; founded in 1990 by five strangers.

Contraband's Corps of Corruption. "At the repeat offenders party, we were referred to as the 'Corpse' of Corruption, but to bastardize a line from Monty Python: 'We ain't dead yet,'" says Chris Everett from Pennsylvania. The Corps arrives mid-October.

Tales from the Naked City

Rich had come down in advance of his bride of 10 years, and was feeling the effects of not being with his lover. He was beside himself. Turns out she had a helluva time getting down to Hedo, being grounded in Miami during a hurricane. After 16 hours, she made it to Hedo around dinnertime. Needless to say, dinner was not top priority on Rich's mind, and they disappeared into their room. The Corps of Corruption didn't let this opportunity go by. We sang at the top of our lungs the Christmas classic "Oh *Come* All Ye Faithful" outside their door until Rich finally emerged with the silliest grin I have ever seen.

—Chris Everett from Pennsylvania

Big repeater months are January, February, mid month to the end of October, and November. Repeat guest percentage average for 1996 was almost 27%. In 1997, Hedo general manager Kevin Levee says the average is closer to one-third. Actual monthly percentage of repeat guest in 1996 were as follows:

January	**36.3%**	July	24.95%
February	31.6%	August	24.95%
March	18.8%	September	19.49%
April	22.5%	**October**	**34.8%**
May	19.5%	**November**	**34.7%**
June	22.7%	December	29.9%

Colorful individuals add to Hedo's flavor

Each week has its bimbo. These are women on their first trip to Hedo and want to make Hedo.

No, that sentence didn't end too fast.

They entertain and give everyone something to talk about. Special thanks go to these memorable women:

92

Carla, the gorgeous nymphet, who sported a huge rock from her new fiancé but didn't want anything to do with him, and asked in the hot tub, as she jumped up and down: "Who wants to fuck me? Who wants to fuck me?" I raised my hand for a laugh, but she looked confused.

Francine of the gigundous torpedo tits was newly married and willing to diddle herself or anyone else on the raft all day long. At the Toga party, she rushed to Joe's penile protuberance made from a 4-in.-diameter Styrofoam pool noodle and said, "I could take that." Everyone believed her.

Caribbean Joy: The slim, pretty 29-year-old with a walk that would make a Slinky envious. She had a personal daily quota of men that she would set each morning to challenge herself.

One night CJ was performing oral sex on a hapless young man lying flat on his back under a spotlight outside the disco. But a coordinator broke up her party and poor CJ burst into tears. She didn't understand; she just wanted to be Miss Hedonism II for the week.

Some women, such as Crazy Mary the younger, sit in the window of Room 1101 right off the volleyball court on the prude beach and call to men to come perform.

Tales from the Naked City

One day on the raft, a girl was allowing all comers to take a throat culture on her. Management asked her to take it to the room so she put a sign in the window: "Free Blow Jobs" and left her door open. Management asked her to stop. She took a Hedo matchbook up to management that has the words: "Now you can experience total freedom." Finally, management told her hotel policy doesn't permit advertising in the windows, but she could leave her door open. I heard the matchbooks are no longer being produced.

Some people at Hedo make themselves memorable by having interesting tattoos and piercings.

One man with more than 40 genital piercings liked to say he made alarms at airports go off so he could drop his trousers in front of everyone. As a professional piercer himself, he decided to perform his art on the beach. Unfortunately, he used rum to cleanse the piercing area and to keep himself lucid and once caught his rubber glove in the piercing of some goofball's foreskin. When he took his hand away: Ouch. The goof's date for the week went home empty-handed.

On Halloween a few years back, Charlie, of the 58-and-counting pieces of silver jewelry on his 70-plus-year-old body, had made a special costume. In addition to a clown wig, he wore two Glo-sticks attached to each nipple piercing, and a Glo-stick attached down below. He told me he started piercing himself in the early 1990s so people would have more reasons to talk to him.

Some people are known by their activities: One guy always does the same dueling glow-in-the-dark nunchacku performance to the song "Dueling Banjos" in the talent show during Toga night.

A guest from Texas wears a cap that says "Older Than Dirt." He won't own up to his age, but he's lived a long life. He puts removable tattoos on the ladies who stand in line for the opportunity.

Other men shave pubic hair in interesting patterns while on the nude beach. Their shop names include Pussy Galore and the Barbers of Negril. They even bring photo books of their work for ladies to choose styles from.

Many guests have nicknames: Cowboy Bob, Ringmon, Biff, Island Dan, Fly Boy Fink, Mom and Dad, Senator (for working the beach), Studman, Towelhead, Rev. JimBob Feelgood, The Legend, and lots of Docs. Women seem to get nicknames only if they are motherly, goofy, or slutty.

Tales from the Naked City

Two couples had befriended each other and the husbands decided to play a trick on their wives. They told an oriental gentleman who lurked around naked and didn't talk to anyone but stared a lot, that their wives wanted to have sex with him. But first they wanted to make sure he had no diseases. The man promptly pulls his mouth wide to show he had no diseases. Seeing he was an idiot, the husbands had him show the inside of his upper and lower lip and tongue, not unlike buying a horse, and they then they made him show his penis. The oriental gentleman spoke with a heavy accent, "See, no disease, no disease!"

The disease-free gentleman was excited and during lunch approached the wives and started stroking their arms and smiling at them. The women, of course, had no idea why he was there, until they asked him why he was acting this way. He told them of the marvelous opportunity the husbands had granted.

Nodding knowingly, the women told the gentlemen that their husbands had played a terrible trick on him. They said they were lesbians and their husbands were homosexuals. When he was supposed to enter the room to make love, the husbands would be coming right behind him with erections. The oriental man began to panic, and just then the husbands returned. Terrified, the man ran away calling out "no sex, no sex."

Other regulars include Jim, the eldest Tilley Bare at age 73; Big Bill the RDOM and his many assistant RDOMs (resident dirty old men); Jamaica Jim (a legend in his own mind); Crazy Mary, a fun-loving woman of the grandmother age bracket (who last time I saw her came to dinner in her exotic push-up bra and panties), Ewenice Ramsbottom (an inflatable sheep), and that screeching Valkyrie who insists "All fat asses get in the pool for aqua-aerobics." (Oh, that's me.)

Horace Goodhue, a Hedo regular known for his properly worn kilts, died July 16, 1997. He was 91. He always smiled as his knees balanced many a 20-year-old who thought he was harmless.

Matt Slovic, the honorary mayor of Hedonism II, comes to Hedo for seven weeks at a time, many times a year. He has mellowed since the old days. But his Heineken parties with a Heineken girl designate still can rev up on the beach on a picnic table. All the labels from the green bottles end up pasted to the girl—sometimes several cases worth.

Matt Slovic, also known as the Mayor, spends about four months of the year total at Hedo and throws Heineken parties on the beach.

"I met Matt on my first trip to Hedo in 1989. He told me that Hedonism II was the last refuge on planet earth for crazy people. He stated in no uncertain terms that there are no rules at Hedonism II. The prude pool was for the nudist whenever the nudists wanted it to be.

He used to enjoy taking off his pants and strutting naked on the main bar whenever anyone dared him to. You will remember that the main bar has been remodeled with a canopy over it. This modification was to keep Matt off the bar. He is too tall to walk up there now.

One of his favorite pastimes was organizing the nude hot tub stuffing events. The photo of 355 people crammed in the tub is still sold by Color Negril. And there's Matt in the back waving to the camera."

—Frank Dumas

The aging of Hedo guests

Hedo realizes the bread-and-butter guest is the repeater, but the repeaters are getting older. To keep these old-coot guests coming back, Hedo could announce the following policy changes and capital improvements, says Paul from New York:

If two guests share the same room, their nurse can stay free.

Oxygen hookups will be available in the dining area (on the columns), in the disco, in the piano bar, and at the beach.

Delroy will serve dirty bananas with Ensure instead of milk.

Dumping stations will be hidden throughout the grounds for those required to wear a bag.

As a true all-inclusive hotel, Hedo will supply a large box of Depends in each room. (Make it crotchless for PJ night.)

The hot tub will have a ramp and be wheelchair accessible.

New beach party games will feature bingo.

Guests may choose to have a meal put through the blender.

At lunchtime spin you won't have to find out the name of the person across from you in the line. You will be asked for your own name...but the person across the line can give you hints.

Instead of Chinese food night, Jamaican night, and lobster night, look for roughage night, vitamin E night, and solid food night.

A wheelchair parade will replace the toga parade. The object is to make your wheelchair look like a Roman chariot.

Bras and jocks will be required on the nude beach because of wheelchairs running over the many body parts dragging on the ground.

The PJ party will be held at three o'clock in the afternoon, before naptime.

Pastafari will serve intravenously.

Doug from Pennsylvania adds to Paul's list:

Scavenger hunt used to find lost prosthetic limbs.

Wet T-shirt contest becomes breast exam clinic.

Massages on nude beach for males also include prostate exam.

Erections clarified to mean new construction projects.

Nude cruise doubles as ash-scattering ceremony.

Choice of vegetables at dinner include guests at table.

Stay of more than three days requires referral from HMO.

Best tan contest bans those receiving radiation and chemotherapy.

Metal detectors available at dive shack. Bermuda shorts with big pockets—extra charge.

Decaf now sold at offshore boats.

Lunchtime spin contest—one-handed truss unfastening.

Black knee-highs for men required apparel at Pastafari (sandals optional).

New slogan adopted—"Be Regular for a Week."

Tales from the Naked City

Sometimes you wonder if you have been at Hedo too long. One early evening a friend and I spot a *USA Today* on the beach just as we note two couples are enjoying themselves in the bay, but we decide that reading the paper is more interesting.

—HedoHenry

Seeing all the body art is part of the fun of Hedo.

People write songs and poems about Hedo

Hedonismville
(to the tune of Jimmy Buffett's "Margaritaville")
By Doug Bowen from West Chester, Pa.

Got off the bus ride
Thought that I might die
From dodgin' that livestock all over the road.
But now I'm at Hedo...I took off my Speedo
And headed to Delroy's to get somethin' cold.

CHORUS:
Wasted away again in Hedonism-ville
Searchin' for a new toga to wear
Some people say that we're all crazy who stay...
But you know...that we just don't care.

Down at the nude beach
My drink within arms' reach
Nothin' to do but lie out on my float.
Feelin' the ripples
Countin' all those nipples!
Hey guys—I think it's time to moon the Sandals boat!

CHORUS

Put on my PJs
Danced to the DJs
Went to that hot tub to check out the sights.
My girl, yeah I brought her;
She went under water,
Ahhh, holy mackerel, I think I'm gettin' a bite!

CHORUS

Back on the airplane—
What the hell's my name?
Got to get back to this thing we call life.
I'll try to remember
To come back in September.
But somethin's still missin'—Oh shit, where's my wife?!

CHORUS

Jamaica
A poem by Horace Goodhue, 1906-1997
reprinted with permission of his widow, Orpha Goodhue

To my good friends, both old and new
I'll sit a while and think of you.
Palms are waving overhead.
From noses to toes I'm getting red!

Busy days with much to do.
Can't do it all—here's just a few:
Water 'robics out of doors
Barefoot dance on polished floors

Here "old-time" dancing is all too slow.
The Reggae beat is all the go.
Starts at 10 and lasts till dawn.
Wait a while and the breakfast's on.

Swim and float along the shore
Or find out what a snorkel's for.
Evening spent at music bars
Or take a walk beneath the stars.

The food bell rings five times a day:
Keep all hunger pains at bay.
I'm sure a week will be enough
Of such a life and fancy stuff.

It's good fun now, but soon will seem
To be a very pleasant dream
In mem'ry's book while sitting there
At home again in my easy chair.

The Hot Tub
Words by Richie, a piano player
(Sung to "Maria" from "West Side Story")

The Hot Tub.
I've just gotten laid in the Hot Tub.
Imagine all the strife
The moment that my wife finds out.

The Hot Tub
We did it right there in the Hot Tub.
My balls will be interred
The moment that the word gets out.

The Hot Tub.
It was such a romantic setting.
Now divorce papers I will be getting.
The Hot Tub.
I'll soon be regretting the Hot Tub.

The most beautiful sex I ever had.
The Hot Tub.

The Hedonism Blues
Words and music by Eric V. Fields

I came here less than a week ago,
Didn't know if the pace was fast or slow,
Went to the hot tub...went to the beach
Nothing seemed out of my reach,
I've seen you in clothes...I've seen you undressed,
Now tell me...which one do you like best,
But one thing I'm feeling and you know that it's true,
I'm starting to feel...the Hedonism Blues.

I went to the island...Ready for fun,
Went around meeting everyone,
Some friends you'll keep and some you will lose,
But you'll never get rid of your Hedonism Blues.

C'mon get naked, c'mon be free,
Get into the insanity,
Open your mind and forget the rules,
Enjoy yourself or you will be a fool,
Cherish this moment for the memory you won't lose,
Especially when you get home...with the Hedonism Blues.

Capt. Bob's Turtles Anthem

We are the Naked Turtles
And we're having lots of fun
Running 'round bare naked
To catch a little sun
You may think that we're perverted
But we've got lots of class
You may not realize it

Every turtle owns an ass.
Dirty words and evil thoughts
Would never be our style,
And asses are our donkeys,
Which aren't considered vile.
Whenever you hear the question
Are you a turtle, mon?
You'll always hear the answer:
You bet your sweet ass I am!

Myrtle, Myrtle, she's a turtle
And she's very, very fertile.
Evil thoughts and dirty words
Will never enter our minds,
And she'll lead us all to heaven
As we ride on our behinds.

Chapter 4

Sex

The Hedo self-proclaimed credos over the years have been: "The pleasure comes in many forms," "The mind, body, spirit, and soul," and "Be wicked for a week." The credo should be "He who hesitates masturbates."

Sex is not as rampant as Hedo's reputation makes it out to be. You must be quick or you could miss an opportunity to see something interesting or act on an offer. You also have to bring your own condoms, and often your own partner. Hedo provides neither.

Single girls do go to Hedo, and this repeater gang proves it.

On July 25, 1997, an article in the *Wall Street Journal* (p. B1) said, "Bookings Boom AGain at 'Adult' Resorts" and portrayed Hedo as a singles paradise by saying: "The swinging-singles resorts of the 70s are making a quiet but curious comeback." Someone who may not know Hedo well wrote this, possibly a first-timer.

Tales from the Naked City

I've known her all these years and never thought that she would do something like that in public. *Said by Jim watching his wife take off her top during the wet T-shirt contest.*

Hedo is not a singles resort. Half the guests are couples. And the sex never slowed or stopped, so it's not making a comeback. Sure, as the 80s turned into the 90s, the attitude of the hotel marketing and staff wasn't naughty, but the guests were still making it with one another. Now the marketing is more lascivious, and the guests are merely still at it.

> "Hedo is fortunately one of the few places in the world that someone can get away with acting on fantasies, whether spontaneous or well thought out, while avoiding the long arm of the do-gooders who feel they should decide everyone's morality levels."
> —Steve from Knoxville, Tenn., married, age 52

Tales from the Naked City

I'm your waiter and you can do whatever you want. *Said to Sue Ann, when she asked if she could remove her jacket and sit in the Pastafari only in her leather and chain top.*

I'm the manager and the jacket stays on. *Said to Sue Ann by the manager of the restaurant.*

Finding partners at Hedo

Many romances start at Hedo, but because of distance at home, don't pan out. But that's not always true. Cissy from California, a well-heeled divorced woman in her early 30s, came to Hedo by herself and had a torrid affair with Larry from Jersey, a tattooed man who smoked, lived with his mother, and was the complete opposite of anything she would date at home. Every day she asked, "What am I doing?" After the trip, he called her at home. Then he drove to California to visit her. Three months later they married.

Lori met Dennis at Hedonism II. Her first words to him were "Can I sit on your raft?" Those words are engraved on the inside of his wedding band—and they've been back to Hedo regularly since.

"On one of our 14 trips to Hedo, I saw the ideal Greek god and immediately went into heat.

My husband said, 'he is probably stuck up.' X was as friendly and as pleasant as can be.

My husband said, 'he probably doesn't have any money.' X was there for a week to rest before he took over his dad's million-dollar dental practice in Miami.

The next day we are playing backgammon on the beach when I look up and see X floating by in all his glory. My husband is staring at me funny. I can't find my dice. My husband politely points to my drink so I can recover them.

The next day my husband takes pictures of X and me nude in the water. Several weeks later he produced a T-shirt with X and me in living color. I am likely the only person in Florida who lives in Palm Beach but goes to Miami to have her teeth cleaned."

—Linda from Florida, age 44

Tales from the Naked City

Things grow on the nude beach. A dark-haired woman is sitting next to a male friend having lunch. Her hand casually rests on his thigh. A ravishing redhead joins them on his other side and notices the hand on the thigh. The competition begins. The redhead fondles the gentleman's balls. Not to be outdone, the brunette grabs his meat.

The gentleman pulls his baseball cap lower over his face and says "Oh boy." Neither woman had been intimate with him before. Other friends join the three for lunch, slowly realizing what is occurring under the table. The gentleman's hands on the table begin to shake. The brunette tells the redhead that it's too dry, so in her classy inimitable way, the redhead spits on it.

Everyone is casually eating sandwiches. One woman said, "He's going to come." A man said, "Just don't hit my lunch with it."

The brunette asks a woman at the table for a plate of mayonnaise. The six people at the table are sitting boy-girl so the plate of condiment was passed and above the table all seemed normal to those walking up to chat. To those lying on nearby beach chairs, however, a six-cylinder engine had been invented.

When looking for a partner, decide if you want a one-nighter or a week-long romance, and pick appropriately. The convenience of choosing someone who is leaving the next day cannot be overestimated. Just because a person isn't a dream come true, he or she can still make a good one-nighter.

Find out when your prospect is leaving before swapping spit, or you might be stuck with a leeching dud by accident. To enjoy your new-found romance for day-time activities, choose someone from your beach (nude or prude).

Generally, young people hang on the prude beach, and older (over 30) hang on the nude beach. Generally, single women on the prude beach get more action than do single women on the nude beach—by choice. Nudes talk more willingly with strangers than Prudes, though. Small consolation, I know.

Lean on the bars to meet people. Just stand there with drink in hand. Small group settings, such as those on the Catamaran or the dive boat, also are good ways to meet folks.

Be available. If someone keeps walking away when you approach, don't follow more than twice. The person is avoiding you.

When all else fails, gentlemen, be aware that local prostitutes do pay for accommodations at Hedo and can be bought (not controlled or condoned by the hotel). One young buck said he had sex for free from a prostitute at Hedo, so he gave her the $50 tip she requested instead—how clever.

How to get laid at Hedo

Women easily meet and catch men because they have the monopoly, and the ratio of men to women provides little competition.

Women also get away with the dumbest conversation topics. Joan from the East Coast comes up with the best ones. Once she surveyed the beach for men with specific qualities, such as nonmatching whorl patterns on thumbs (which of course means you are gay according to the *National Enquirer* article she carried around with her).

Testing for broken butt hairs by lightly caressing the men's behinds is another favorite conversation starter. A lot of takers for that one.

You also can walk the beach (hot tub at cocktail hour is good for this game, too) in search of statistics for a "Which Ball Hangs Lower Survey." My stats are 60% left low, 30%

right low, and 10% dead even. Naturally, you'll have to fluff them and get them at face level to take a true reading.

The best T-shirt seen on a woman (thank you, Marilyn):

If you can't
make me
laugh,
think, or
come...
FUCK OFF

Men have a tougher time getting laid because the ratio of women to men is low, making the odds go up for the women not to choose you.

"Don't push. Ease into the scene. The ladies at Hedo are the same who left the States. Nothing mysterious happens when they walk into Hedo that makes them insatiable nymphos. Hedo is a beautiful place where relationships can accelerate from the party atmosphere and constant companionship. When was the last time you spent 24 hours straight on a first date?

"Stay in a cognitive state, not exactly sober but not obnoxiously loud and drunk. Do what you would do here in the States to meet women who interested you. They are there for a good time, too, but not necessarily a sexually good time (unless they really like you). Here are some hints:

Get to know them. Take an interest in their minds as much or more than their bodies or your horniness.

Learn something about them so when you see them again you remember something you can talk about to start the conversation again. Learn their state, city, or whatever. Then if you forget the name you can always say "Hey, Minnesota!"

Treat everyone with respect: don't brag about materialistic things such as cars, job, etc., because they don't mean a thing in the islands. The Benz ain't there."

—Chris Everett from Pennsylvania

Here are my secrets for scoring at Hedo. Look! The rules are just like in the real world.

Physical tips. Don't stare. Staring makes you look like a weirdo with sick fantasies that most women likely don't want to be part of. On the beach wear dark wraparound glasses.

Don't grab or touch a woman who is not openly inviting your touch. If you must touch, use the flat of your hand on her arm gently between her elbow and shoulder. Too many men think that because a woman is dancing near-naked in front of them, they can grab—at Hedo they can't.

Let her catch you checking her out, but only for a moment, then act embarrassed for getting caught. Only do that once. Women also use this technique to attract the attention of men.

Don't travel in packs of more than you and your buddy. You don't exude confidence or originality in a pack. (Unless you are all performing together—then that's cool.) Mingle— this is a 24-hour cocktail party.

Don't assume that because a woman is playing grab-ass with every man you see her with that you can get in on the action too. She might have known them all for years (or at least

10 minutes), and this is their fun, not yours—unless invited. The show might be good to watch at least.

Words to say and not say. Don't walk up and immediately ask, "Where are you from?" Who cares? That's a boring introduction and everyone says it. Names are more important. On vacation, the last thing people want to talk about is home.

Ask about a situation you see going on and make the excuse that this is new to you but you are interested in learning more as a curious bystander. Never be judgmental of the trashy-looking broad with her foot on the bar. The woman you are hitting on might be amused it. Hedo is about different strokes for different folks.

Offer interesting information to women. Women like gossip. And Hedo is the place where everyone learns everything about everybody and tells everyone else, which is something to take seriously. The staff talks and guests talk. Guests spread rumors all the time for lack of better occupation. One year I was a lesbian. The next year, asexual. Then I finally made the rank of slut. What a banner year.

Fool the woman into believing you just want to talk to her. That gives her the opportunity to let you know when the time's ripe for more. Face it, women are the ones who lead this dance.

Never make sexual or repetitious complimentary remarks about a woman until you are in bed with her or definitely heading in that direction. Too many men think many physical compliments are the way to a woman's heart. You can tell her—as you keep your eyes on her face—that she's smart, clever, interesting, wild, or whatever. You can mention once that her outfit was an excellent choice and grin. Don't dwell on her body, face, beauty in public, only do that in pubic, I mean, when you are having carnal knowledge.

If you are sweet on a gal, find out which guy she talks with. Be *his* buddy. Things will happen. Befriend those men, and they then vouch for your wholesomeness as part of the gang.

112

Be careful about being obvious when using this technique. And don't dump the men when you finally meet the woman.

Don't act so bloody thrilled when you get to hang with women. Friendly is good. Remember—fool the woman—only show your passion when scoring or in that obvious verbal dance that leads to imminent scoring.

Don't assume any relationships a woman may or may not have. Never ask about a husband or boyfriend to "qualify" a woman. Are you shopping for a wife? At Hedo? Please. (Actually many people have found the loves of their respective lives, but still.) If she wants you, she'll let you know.

If a woman has a boyfriend or husband, she still might want you, unless she's using it as a brush-off line. Also, don't assume because she's chumming with other guys that they are scoring with her or that she won't score with you too.

Your clothes. Don't wear a gold chain around your neck if you are young, muscular, and less than 6 feet. Chains add to a Vinnie look. Fight back and be better than that. Look dapper or casual instead.

Don't wear your jams to the nude beach. Men look silly covered from above navel to knees. At most wear a Speedo so gals can check out your assets. When Nudes go to the prude beach, they have the decency to vaguely cover up. Prudes should vaguely uncover on the nude beach.

Button-down shirts are dapper, but don't wear one that would go under a suit coat. If you have a big belly, untuck your shirt over jeans or twill shorts. T-shirts on chubby guys make them look sloppy—unless they have a killer saying on it that makes them endearing to women because of their humor. And leave the polyester at home, please. Wear cotton—the rooms have irons, use them.

Wear clothes that fit. Too tight on a less than slim figure or too loose on any physique is not appealing to a woman.

Make sure your sneakers are in good repair. Deck shoes or sandals are fine. Avoid dress shoes—unless you are wearing a jacket and leaving the campus (leave quickly to avoid the embarrassment of being overdressed).

Now the bitter truth. Some guys follow all the tips, are befriended by every woman on the beach, and still can't score. They are focusing on women who wouldn't want to score with them because of age, looks, or values that have nothing to do with the guy. Short, chubby, homely, boring, single men get laid at Hedo, but seldom regularly. Just like at home.

Social protocol is social protocol. And mating rituals are mating rituals. The conversation and activities at Hedo are just bawdier and access is easier.

Women: How to reject pickup lines

Man: So, wanna go back to my place?
Woman: I don't know. Will two people fit under a rock?

Man: Haven't we met before?
Woman: Yes, I'm the receptionist at the VD Clinic.

Man: I'd really like to get into your pants.
Woman: No, thanks. There's already one asshole in there.

A man in his 60s approaches a 20-something with "Where have you been all my life?" She took one glance at him and said, "For the first half of it, I probably wasn't born yet."

Man: Hey, come on, we're both here at this bar for the same reason.
Woman: Yeah! Let's pick up some chicks!

Man: Haven't I seen you someplace before?
Woman: Yes. That's why I don't go there anymore.

Man: I'd like to call you. What's your room number?

Woman: It's at the front desk.

Man: But I don't know your last name.

Woman: That's at the front desk too.

Tales from the Naked City

Two men and one woman were enjoying the fornicatorium one day (covered by the veil of water). Halfway through, they decide to move their threesome four feet to the other side of the fornicatorium to accommodate their next activity. The three hear the scraping of many lounge chairs as people scramble for better positions of viewing. Someone later told the woman that she was heard moaning. "That wasn't me!" she said, "My mouth was full!"

Men: Don't use these pickup lines

1. Your name must be Daisy, because I have an incredible urge to plant you right here.

2. Just call me milk—I'll do your body good.

3. That dress looks becoming on you, but if I were on you, I'd be coming too.

4. Is that Windex? I can see myself in your pants.

5. I'm sorry, I thought that was a Braille name tag.

6. Excuse me, do you have your room number, I seem to have lost mine.

7. I'm new here. May I have directions to your room?

8. Fuck me if I'm wrong, but is your name Yolanda?

9. I love every bone in your body—especially mine.

10. The word for the night is legs, let's go back to my room and spread the word.

Alternative sex stuff happens

At Hedo, all types come out to play. Most of the traditional perversions, though, are behind closed doors, except when Master Spike and Slave Joey, the dungeon residents of Room 2180, tied up a young tattooed couple over a tree and gave a spanking demonstration at the hot tub one night.

Bondage is big, big, big at Hedo these days. It's even a category in the PJ party contest.

Tales from the Naked City

A couple had won first place for best bondage outfit at the Pyjama party. Being tuckered, they went back to their room to crash and burn. Two hours later someone knocked on the door and yelled, "Is this where the S&M party is being held?" The couple yelled, "No!" The knocker called back, "Why not?"

At Hedo, I met an articulate, intelligent, and humorous woman who likes to dress like a pony and wins competitions for wearing a bridle and bit, hooves without heels, and a butt plug with a horse's tail as she pulls a small cart. You likely know someone at home who does this too in secret, but at Hedo you learn about it.

I found an index card on the sidewalk with the following instructions (spelling has been fixed):

Blindfold guest wife
D is Down
Give the key back to her
Judge lingerie
Find your panties
Pee on his foot.

I don't get it, and I probably don't want to get it, but it's yet another example of the uniquely Hedo experience.

Ewenice Ramsbottom (in white) finds friends on the beach.

The opportunity for group sex or sex outside your marriage is higher at Hedo than at home, unless you belong to a sex club. Think of Lifestyle weeks as Hedo with an exclamation point. If you find open intimacy offensive then don't go. The Lifestylers love a good time—only part of which is sex. Even if you don't do the same things, it's a great time to go.

Voyeurism and exhibitionism: the Hedo way of life

Perverts. Hedo makes everyone into childlike perverts. And is it fun!

Many find special joy in watching others perform sexual acts. Some Hedo guests prefer to catch the participants at the act rather than to have the act forced upon viewing range. They want to feel as though they're getting away with something.

Especially grand is seeing couples in the water on their rafts. They feel so private out there. But everyone *is* watching. They'll even applaud and talk about you with smiles if you appear to be trying to be discreet or embarrassed.

Tales from the Naked City

A woman was watching a couple mating on a raft in the ocean. "They're disgusting," she said.

I asked, "Then why do you keep watching." She replied, "I'm just waiting for them to stop."

Guests from beyond the nude beach are voyeurs too. They even come from other hotels to watch. One time the Sandals boat, passing Hedo's nude beach, slowed to a crawl to let people gawk—three or four big guys all went to one side of the boat, and it tipped so much, one of the guys fell in.

Exhibitionism has its place at Hedo too. Sometimes guests have scheduled events. A growing number of public sexual displays are occurring at Hedo. If seen, the staff or the guards ask you to stop, especially in the dining area or around the disco.

"I do not condone or permit open sex in public areas. It is crude and vulgar," says Hedo's general manager Kevin Levee. "Some staff, however, are not as vigilant as others. I want to bring it under control. Hedonism II is like a race horse. We need to reign it in occasionally so it doesn't burn out."

Activities inside your room are your own business. If you leave your curtains open, however, people will watch. And if you leave your door open, they will also watch. Partially open doors generally are an invitation to look and not touch.

Tales from the Naked City

We had a friend who was into window-shopping. Every night he would walk the beach and see what action he could see inside different rooms. Finally, one night I agreed to go with him around 11. We go walking and all of a sudden see some action going on in a room. We stop and watch and just see three naked backsides on the bed. He is getting interested and I am goading him. Finally, I knock on the window and up pops three faces—a couple we were friendly with—and the peeping Tom's wife. The shocked look on his face changed after we all broke up laughing. He knew he had been had.

—HedoHenry

Teasing and innuendo are great at Hedo, but the overt sex—where people are actually getting off in the daylight in public areas—goes overboard some weeks. Other weeks, guests walk around wondering where the action is.

The amount of open sex is a balancing act. Few people want to eat their cheeseburger on the same picnic table where they just watched someone perform oral sex to completion. Some don't care. Hedo's rep could fall into gross instead of interesting. Even perverts have ideas on what's over the line at Hedo.

On the second floor as you walk near Room 2269 or so, you can see off into the garden to a concrete table and bench. At ground level, trees and bushes block the view. Sometimes couples are busy there who don't realize they are being watched till you let them know with wild applause.

You also can peer through the bathroom louvers of Room 1101 as you walk toward the nude beach rooms down the sloped path from the dining area. I once saw two young bucks jumping up and down on their beds singing along with their tape of the Monkee's "Last Train to Clarksville."

Tales from the Naked City

I'm sitting on the toilet and hear a man's and woman's quiet voices outside my bathroom louvers. I don't move in my desperate bid to overhear them. I hear kissing, giggling, and heavy breathing and feel terribly naughty. I hear no sound for about a minute, and then my roommate walks in. I tell her what I had heard and how I caught them. She gives me one of those looks and rolls her eyes and says, "That was me, you idiot."

Sexual openness doesn't extend to gay men

Unfortunately, some people at Hedo have personal problems with the gay community and do not welcome them. So much for free spirits and open minds. Even the Jamaicans tend to shun homosexuals. I don't recommend gay guys go to Hedo to be open. If you are discreet, though, you are fine.

Tales from the Naked City

Beware the floating penis. Two well-hung male friends were standing in the hot tub and chatting close together when they each looked down and realized, to their horror, that their genitals were nose to nose. Like North Pole meeting North Pole, they bounced apart.

Hedo hosts many gay people—more than you know, just like in the real world. Bi-curious or bisexual men also can find pleasures at Hedo. The openness is just not there as it is with other types of sexuality.

Tales from the Naked City

Can I cornrow your pubic hair? *A gay man's attempt to pick up a bi-curious, single man.* Got a good laugh, but didn't succeed.

The lesbian, bisexual, and bi-curious women are welcome compared with gay men because straight men like to watch gals together, and they keep hoping for an invitation that never comes.

Since 1985, I've only heard of or seen one case of a gay man hitting on a married man in an obtrusive fashion. The guard took the drunken gay man away. Gay men don't hit on heteros at Hedo—they come down with their partners or use their gaydar to look for other gay men—discreetly.

Chapter 5

Entertainment in this land beyond Kansas

Find out what the time is. Although events usually run on island time ("soon come"), sometimes they do start on time. If you are five minutes late for an event, such as a bicycle ride, find an entertainment coordinator. The staff might have thought no one wanted to play because no one was there on time.

The hotel has no clocks (unless the room alarm clocks come back). During winter Jamaica matches Eastern Standard Time and during summer it's Central. Jamaica doesn't have Daylight Savings as in the United States.

Entertainment coordinators, similar to Club Med's G.O.s, are the young people who live on campus, work 20 hours a day, and are supposed to lead guests into temptation but deliver them from evil. Their turnover is high, so the odds of seeing the same one next year are low.

Late each night a coordinator writes a list of the next day's activities on the chalkboard located between the dining area and front desk. On another nearby chalkboard, events in Spanish are listed.

Bastardizing the activity board is fun. The natural fashion show becomes *un*natural and body painting becomes *truck* painting (the hillbillies go wild for that one). Times are listed for golden showers, group orgy, and phone sex too. Have chalk, will travel.

"You can tour, shop, do water sports, read, relax, workout in the weight room, play the big chessboard in the square, eat, drink, swim, do island cruises or body painting, drink, eat, drink, meet new people, drink, learn about Jamaica, tour Grand Lido, go across to the 'straw market,' drink, chat, go into Negril, go to Rick's Café for lunch, drink, go snorkeling, drink some more, take a nap, get up and drink, find your wife, *stop* drinking, bicycle into town, take the nature walk, learn how to do the trapeze, go sailing, walk the beach to see other resorts, join a game of shuffleboard, drink Ting, tell a joke, tell a lie, tell the Prudes to go back to their own beach, laze around on a raft, go fishing, drink some new concoction of Delroy's—come to think of it, there isn't much to do, but damn, I need a nap after just thinking about the little there is to do."

—Chris Everett from Pennsylvania
a.k.a. Hedoman, age 45

What was once set in stone for a dozen years has been changing: the schedule of events. Pyjama party is still on Tuesday, and Toga night is still on Thursday, but other events are more variable than in the past.

Chinese dinner night has most recently been moved to Wednesday, after the repeater party, which is still at 6:30 p.m. Wednesdays. The Island Picnic only goes to Booby Cay Wednesdays now. Lobster night, when served, is Tuesday, not Saturday. Monday still has 50s-60s dancing after dinner, but Elvis only sings every other week. Body painting and the best tan contest on the nude beach are now variable, instead of Tuesday and Friday events.

Hedo no longer gives tokens for prizes. Now you earn Hedo Bucks to be cashed in for prizes such as booze or SuperClubs-imprinted merchandise such as coffee mugs or key chains. Occasionally a bottle of booze is a prize, like in the old days (when your luggage was weighed down with bottles on the way home).

These prize winners have fun being painted, but removing the paint is even more fun.

Daytime land games and sports

The hotel has tons of land sports, such as badminton, bocci ball, nude and prude shuffleboard, basketball (good for nude "horse"), nude and prude volleyball, bicycling, and Ping-Pong.

The two air-conditioned squash courts are seldom busy. Sometimes a visiting pro is in residence. The courts never close so you can play at all hours. The ambiance isn't good for a rendezvous, though; the light is bright and the benches are hard.

The six tennis courts are lit for night play, and resident pros hold clinics twice daily and tournaments.

People sweat in the fitness center and during aerobics classes. That's nice. Most people, though, are on vacation from the reality of their burgeoning flesh. Hedo plans to build an air-conditioned facility.

The circus workshops feature flying and swinging trapeze, trampoline clinics, juggling, tightrope walking, unicycle, and bicycle balancing acts.

The land games are more fun than the land sports for those not athletically inclined. They include the daily lunchtime spin games ("the lunchtime spank"), best tan contest, beach Olympics, arts and crafts, body painting on the nude beach, and more. One man in the natural fashion show wore a "Hard Rock Jock," which was a real rock. Talk about getting your rocks off.

Tales from the Naked City

Goat races with live farm animals resulted in naked bejeweled women and men coaxing recalcitrant pygmy goats, with names like White Cloud, Puff, and Brand X, down the beach and back up again. Written rules stated no one could lift, drag, push, or masturbate the animals to encourage forward progress. The rules were ignored, especially by that woman wearing the rubber gloves, who was whispering to Charmin.

Drew from Toronto and Oliver from West Chester, Pa., take part in the natural fashion show on the nude beach.

Lunchtime spin reverberates

Every day about 1:45 p.m. lunchtime spin takes place in the dining area. These contests include the weekly wet T-shirt competition, music trivia, and other pseudo-naughty pass-the-baton-type games. They are all fun and silly and break up the day. If you are modest, wear a garment that covers your crotch from below because some games require interesting angles.

Some coordinators haven't mastered microphone volume control yet and also play the rigorous music to ensure your dog at home can hear it. For a quiet lunch, eat early or late or on the beach.

Once a week some women dance in wet T-shirts for the men (some weeks, only if the staff can con the women into it). In return, another day focuses on the men with the Body Motion contest, where the men dance clothed (if the ladies allow them to remain that way). Before the event begins, the coordinators ask the ladies seated along the recessed stage what attributes they'd like to see from the men. Many answer tight buns, good moves, pumped pecs, and so on. One woman said, "Men who put the toilet seat down."

A lunchtime spin game prompts some people to find interesting places to position the blow-job shot (real liquor) for drinking.

Tales from the Naked City

During lunchtime spin, the coordinator asked a woman, "What's the craziest thing you've done since you arrived at Hedonism II?" She replied, "I gave a guy a blow job." Small applause. Typical stuff. The coordinator asked the woman next to her the same question. Her response was: "Watching that girl giving a blow job to my husband." Big applause.

Island Picnic produces drunken boys and girls

The Island Picnic usually consists of young guys dying to see the tits of the four or five single women who go. This varies of course (quantities of women). But any first-timer under age 40 (especially the Prudes) thinks the Island Picnic is a laugh-riot. The coordinator leading the picnic makes a difference on whether fun is had.

Many people get drunk and naked on the Island Picnic. No one has to get drunk or naked, but what's the point in going otherwise? To stay sober and dressed, don't play the reindeer games.

The boat for the Island Picnic leaves the pier at 10:30 a.m. on Wednesdays to go to the island of the Booby Cay (in Jamaica pronounced boo-bi-kee) just off shore. The coordinators lead games for a couple hours in the water at the edge of the beach, and then lunch is served on the grill there. Bread, salad, and chicken never taste so good as after drinking all morning. Drinks usually include rum punch, soda, and beer. Everybody is usually back to Hedo by 2:30 p.m. to crash and burn on the beach in a fit of giggles.

"If you haven't done the picnic, you have to try it. It's a ton of drinking, which I'm not up for, and tons of fun games too. The group that went consisted of at least 75% nudists, and we had fun getting everyone else naked too. A single guy from Canada enjoyed a few of the 'kiss the body' games. How I got paired up with him is beyond me, but I hope he enjoyed himself. The food on the picnic was great and a big welcome after several hours of playing in the water. The next morning we learned the video from our Island Picnic was so graphic that Color Negril didn't have enough footage to sell after editing. Needless to say, our group bought the unedited version.

—Suanne from St. Somewhere, age 36

A source of pride: winning the best tan contest

White lines on nude bodies attest that some places are difficult to tan. Look for smile lines under buttocks, a.k.a. "tail lights"; the smiles of white under breasts, a.k.a. "headlights"; and those two white lines on a lady's pelvic area, a.k.a. "lane dividers." Best tan contestants often lift arms and boobs to demonstrate the excellence of their tanning technique.

Worst tan or white butt contestants weasel their way into the competition and often win a prize too. Tanning is an obsession for some Nudes; others stay under the many trees and become the judges of this weekly event.

One woman's husband liked to work with deer leather and produced for her the most charming tanning contraption: a labia separator to hold her lips apart for better sun access. Visualize two soft-leather-clad mousetraps gently clamped to left and right lips of labia majora with strings attached to strap them to the thighs so the mousetraps stay apart.

A spool also makes an excellent butt separator. Many want to put in an order for breast and cheek lifters.

Tales from the Naked City

A rich man from the Midwest who likes to buzz the beach with his piloted Lear jet before touching down in MoBay brought a global positioning system (GPS) device to Hedo. His friends didn't know what it was, but they did know it had the right size batteries for their vibrator, which had gone dead. Oops. Time to reprogram the GPS.

Water sports beyond muff diving

Hedo offers diving, snorkeling, and water skiing. For para-sailing, walk far down the beach and pay for it. Aqua-aerobics in the nude and prude pool are often scheduled. The wind-surfing equipment is fairly worn but useable. Hedo has both Hobie Cats and Sunfish sailboats, and if you are gone too many hours, the staff comes looking for you.

To enjoy marine life without getting wet, toss bread off the end of the pier just before sunset, when many colorful fish come out.

Daily dives make Hedo cost-effective

Divers come to Hedo, not for the incredible underwater views (they're average) but for the daily dives included in the hotel's rate. Jamaica is not known as a prime location for diving, but it can be wonderful. Don't expect the views found in the B.V.I., Caymans, Cozumel, and Aruba, though.

You can have a good dive experience if you understand the risks and are willing to assume them. The diving is safe, but as all good divers know, you are always on your own and safety is in your own hands. The dive master won't lead you to unsafe places.

"We completed our NAUI scuba certification several months before coming to Hedo, so we asked if we could refresh our skills in the pool. The scuba staff said we'd do fine without it.

We made our open dive and were a bit uneasy with the dive master and his predive protocol, but everything went fine and we had a great time."

—Gene from Los Angeles

A friend always brings hard candies onto the boat for his dry mouth after diving. He gives them to all women who show him their tits.

Part of the diving experience is getting in and out of the new 40-foot-long dive boat. It's fast, with its twin 250-hp outboard engines, but it's not diver friendly for access. It has racks for 20 tanks, but space is needed for the dive master and photographer.

> "We really liked the new dive boat. It's fast so you can get to some great virgin sites quickly. True, the tank setup limits the number of people, but we enjoy dives in smaller groups. With too many people you are all over each other. We did not have a problem with the tanks, just pick them up, strap it on, and jump in. With the ladder set up, we just climbed out of the water and took off the equipment in the boat. We think the dive staff at Hedo is great."
>
> —Vicki from Las Vegas

What you'll see. Most dives are drift dives through coral formations with a couple of dives to wrecks (tugboat and drug runner plane). Sometimes you'll see turtles, barracuda, rays, eels, sea snakes, and the occasional nurse shark (learn the hand signal for "big fucking shark").

The water is usually clear with 80-plus feet of visibility. It's about 82° F at 60 feet. Ask the crew to go past Grand Lido to Mike's reef to see lots of fish, virgin reef, sea turtles, and giant stingray.

Usually the dive master takes the boat to a different location every day or takes you to the same place and calls it by a different name. The shallow dives tend to show more wildlife and colors. A person from Color Negril, a photography company, sometimes makes a video of the dive that you can buy later for around $40.

About two years ago *Skin Diver* rated Negril's "Treasure Room," a coral area that is not overly impressive in the day, as one of the top 10 night dives in the Caribbean. The Negril Scuba Center in town can schedule a night dive for you. Bring your own lights, though, as they are rare commodities. They might also be good trading material. The Hedo dive master also does a night dive if several people are interested. The night dives at Hedo are about $35 U.S. and worth it.

Dive schedule. Sign up early for dives each day or the day before because space on the boats is limited.

Three dives are scheduled daily:

9 or 9:30 a.m.: 90-foot dive with 25 minutes' bottom time

11 or 11:30: a.m.: 60-foot dive with 40 minutes' bottom time

1:30 or 2:30 p.m.: Dive at 30 to 45 feet

You can do two one-tank dives per day at Hedo: one early in the day to 60 feet and one in the afternoon. If you want to do both morning dives, the dive master may bend the rules if the second dive isn't full and your dive profile doesn't exceed safety considerations.

Gear. Hedo has all the essential dive equipment you need. BCs, regulators, fins, masks, snorkels, and weights are free to use. None of the regulators have computers. All dives are timed dives. The equipment, mostly USDiver, ranges from acceptable to good. Hedo doesn't have lights or cameras.

Many divers bring their own masks, snorkels, fins, and tropical wet suits (the water feels chilly by the end of a long dive).

Training. No one checks your dive logs. To be able to dive, just show your NAUI or PADI certification cards, fill out a basic questionnaire, and sign a release once at the start of the week. Advanced divers must go through a 30-foot check-out dive before going on the deeper dives if they have not dived at Hedo before.

The resort offers dive instruction at no cost that takes about a half a day. This club certification allows you to go on the shallow dives only. Hedo also has certified PADI instructors for full certification training as an added charge.

PADI training takes a whole week at the Negril Scuba Center, which picks you up at the hotel. Call PADI at 714-540-7234. Call Negril Scuba Center at 876-957-4425 or 876-957-0212.

Tales from the Naked City

During a snorkel trip on the reef, several boats were tied near each other from several resorts, including ours from Hedo. Half the Hedo snorkelers were nude or topless, in the case of the women. A male-female pair of snorkelers from one of the other boats became disoriented while swimming and mistakenly climbed onto our boat. They took off their fins and masks and looked around. Then they saw all of us nude and seminude people. The woman shrieked loudly, and the man was so shocked he slipped and fell back into the water. The woman continued screaming as though a shark chased her. She tried not to look as she gathered her gear to swim back to the right boat. Our stomachs hurt we laughed so hard.

—Denny Pasternak, Omaha, Neb.

Snorkeling outside the hot tub

Right off the beaches (especially the nude beach in the morning) at Hedo and Grand Lido you'll find good snorkeling with clear water and a many types of fish and corals.

The dive shack has snorkeling gear (mask, snorkel, and fins). Be careful of boats in the pier area, and stay within the buoys elsewhere.

The water sports staff also can recommend good local boaters who take you to distant nice spots for U.S. currency, or try to barter with T-shirts and caps brought from home.

Do not take, kill, or touch any water animals. Spear fishing is illegal in Jamaican waters and dangerous to other snorkelers. Many animals will sting or bite you in defense. To bring home a souvenir starfish, buy one.

Catamaran cruises—Nude and Prude

A catamaran docks at Hedo but is a separate business so it's not included in the Hedo rate. Jennifer usually runs the cruises, but Patty and Philip still own the business. Try the trapeze in the front of the catamaran to dip in the ocean and be splashed.

The boat holds maybe 80 people tops, or as many as are willing to pay the $40 or so to board. It includes all drinks.

The day trip goes to the caves where "20,000 Leagues Under the Sea" was filmed. You can cliff jump if desired, but catamaran folks discourage it because someone reportedly broke his back a few years ago. If you do not enter the water right from 30-some feet, the slap of the water could bruise you.

A sunset catamaran cruise to Rick's let's you go ashore. At Rick's the cliffs are up to 40 feet high. Some brazen souls are always jumping. This restaurant-bar provides the best way to see the sunset.

Enjoy a water slide at the Pickled Parrot and its rope that goes into the sea. The restaurant-bar also provides fins and masks for snorkeling.

Evening entices people more than the day

Some evenings Hedo honors special occasions. Every Valentine's Day people dress in red, and one lucky person who goes on stage during dinner wins some complimentary nights at Hedo. Jamaican holidays also receive special tribute. On the U.S. Thanksgiving, which is attended by the self-proclaimed unloved and unwashed crowd, paper turkeys pasted to the stage and columns commemorate the day, and the dining area serves turkey, gravy, and mashed potatoes for dinner.

The biggest hoopla at Hedo is likely its two-day event the evening of Halloween and November 1, the hotel's anniversary, when the Miss Hedonism II pageant is held. That week, Hedo goes all out to show its guests they are appreciated. All guests receive gifts, and repeat guests with high numbers of trips receive even fancier gifts.

On Halloween, guests dress in costume (sexy to scary to silly), and many perform on stage to win complimentary nights at Hedo. Some guests orchestrate whole stage shows with taped music and choreographed steps.

When the first prize was a T-shirt and a Bob Marley record, the contest was less tense. In 1997, less than half the crowd was in costume. Some skits were excellent, but the show lasted past midnight so most of the audience fizzled.

Similarly, the Miss Hedo contest the next night lasts a long time. This pageant of Hedo guests takes about three days of the women's vacations to prepare for. But each contestant receives a minimum of three complimentary nights. Any woman can be in the pageant. The costumes are Las Vegas and the aura Miss America. The duties of being Miss Hedo are nonexistent.

For both evenings, many people seem so intent on winning complimentary days they forget they came to have fun. But the spectacle is truly to be experienced at least once.

Dank disco draws denizens by the dozen

The disco opens at 11:00 p.m. and stays open until the last guest leaves. The disco plays techno-club music—typical American play list. Occasionally the DJs throw in some oldies and Motown in a mix format, but that's rare. The disco, which will be completely renovated in a couple years, is currently cramped, smoky, and hot. It's where the single guys go to pick up girls and vice versa.

Tales from the Naked City

On my first trip to Hedo I went to the disco just before midnight. I sat down and a couple from Ft. Lauderdale joined me. They were on their last night. They put a camera on the table. We talked awhile. They had left the 4- and 6-year-old behind with Grandma and Grandpa.

My watch beeps on the hour and it did. He asked "Is it midnight?" Yes, it was. He told her, "It's time. Get a good one." He disappeared then reappeared in the disco window that reveals the depths of the swimming pool. He provided full frontal nudity. She took the picture.

Then she asked me to take a picture. They both posed naked under water. All the while, the disco crowd cheered.

Then they came down in a more compromising position. Took the pictures.

—Chris from NW Chicago suburbs

Piano bar piques persons of prurient passions

Veronica's piano bar (eponymous for one of its well-loved bartenders) on the court next to the shops and the oversize chessboard is open 6:30 p.m. to 2 a.m. Around 10 p.m. Mondays and Tuesdays, karaoke starts, which can be painful or goofy. Other days, a piano player starts a sing-along.

This respite from the disco provides a comfortable place to sit and listen to fellow guests. The tempo of the evening there varies depending on who's singing and the mood of the piano player. Naked dancing girls on the piano are no longer unusual.

Repeaters will remember Lenworth Ultimate, the short, bald genius of the keys who transposed music to anyone's key, even the key of flat. He occasionally shows up but is no longer a fixture.

When in the piano bar, make sure you know the words to "New York, New York" and "Piano Man." You'll also do best to know the words to these songs because they are played nearly every night:

"Blue Suede Shoes"	"Proud Mary"
"Great Balls of Fire"	"Rockin' Robin"
"Hey Jude"	"Rocky Top"
"Johnny B. Goode"	"Stand by Me"
"Lean on Me"	"Summer Love"
"Let It Be"	"Sweet Caroline"
"Lion Sleeps Tonight"	"Twist & Shout"
"Mack the Knife"	"Under the Boardwalk"
"My Way"	"You've Lost that Loving Feeling"

If one more woman sings "The Rose," "Memory," or "Over the Rainbow," I'll puke. I'll listen to "Summertime" once more though.

Pyjama party: Frederick's of Hollywood comes alive

Every Tuesday night at 11 p.m. the disco starts to fill with men and women in sexy underclothes, pajamas, and goofy outfits. If the crowd is especially huge, Hedo holds the party in the dining area, which, while cooler in temperature, spreads the event out a little too much for any focus.

At the Pyjama party any bedclothes are a go, especially if they are revealing. The Prudes have fun playing like they are risqué, and the Nudes enjoy raising their own blood pressure by slightly covering up.

You can go naked to the PJ party and no one will care. Well, they might, but only in the best sense. I highly recommend standing buck naked at the disco bar in high heels to experience rapture.

Open request to all men: Please stop wearing boxers to PJ night. Gals need entertainment too. Men don't go to the party to see women in camisoles covered by robes.

The glaring lights of some guests' video cameras at PJ night are disconcerting but vaguely avoidable. Color Negril no longer videotapes during PJ or Toga night, ostensibly to protect guest privacy—a growing issue of concern.

Guests' costumes are judged (pseudo-secretly) as they walk in the disco by the coordinators taking names outside the door. If they don't ask your name, you don't win. If they do ask your name, you might have won. Categories vary and can include sexiest, best couple, most naked, most appealing, most original, and best bondage. The competition winners are usually announced at about 1 a.m. so guests mill about and sweat for two hours and often leave after they see who won.

Toga party: No sheet, no eat

Toga party on Thursday night is amusing if you have never hung out, literally, in a bed sheet. Toga night is an opportunity for lighter packing. The hotel provides the evening attire. Pins, belts, and knots hold these white monstrosities together. People come to dinner in their sheets, often tugging this way and that as they adjust and fumble what looked better in the room before they actually moved.

Don't wear underpants or bras underneath like in "Animal House." This evening is 42 steps beyond that scene. Go to the toga tying lessons on Thursday afternoon to learn ideas and techniques.

Tales from the Naked City

One of my best memories is walking to dinner and having my toga fall off, then rewrapping and not moving at all during dinner—then not wanting to take place in the conga line, where togas were falling off left and right.

—Steve Podolak from Smyrna, Del.

Butt cheeks can show and so can tits. Many men flash their genitals all night. Some wear extended organs. Woman can show zero, one, or two breasts—which might be ornamented on the nipples with clips or tassels.

Bring glitter, tinsel garlands, or big honking gold jewelry to garnish your toga. Many people grab flowers and leaves off trees or bring fake garlands for their heads. Arm bands are cool too.

One way to tie the toga is rolling the sheet tightly—starting at one corner to make a long rope—and wrapping it in sexy ways. This leaves little sheet to cover the body, but you can tie two together to make an extra-long rope wrap.

The front desk has sheets available after 7 p.m. To procure an extra one (or your first one if the maid forgot to leave one on your bed or the one you received was icky), just lie and say you didn't get one on your bed.

After dinner everyone suffers through or enjoys the guest and staff talent night, which is a pleasant surprise or a dismal failure. And while the guests are all thrilled that Paul from the staff has learned to sing so well since Hedo became Hedo, they wish more guests had talent because he often sings four songs in a row to fill time on stage.

Next the actual Toga party begins. The staff gathers guests into a long conga line of bouncing, sweaty bodies that snakes through the dining area picking up toga-wearing people.

After many chants and general whoop-whoops, the toga competition begins. Depending on the week, the categories include sexiest, most Roman, worst tied, most virginal, best couple, and most naked. Anyone is welcome on stage to be judged and audience applause determines winners.

A few people leave their togas on to go to the disco or piano bar afterward, but many change into their own clothes.

Hedo's general manager Kevin Levee says the number of people mating on the beach after the Toga party is higher than most nights.

Tales from the Naked City

After a libidinous evening in the hot tub, two swing couples who had just met learned that the husbands had complementary fields of endeavor: one wrote software, one installed systems. After enjoying conviviality, the men wrote up a $2 million contract bedside for a business deal once they returned home.

Drugs are illegal and plentiful

Breathe in that sweet smell in the air. Could be Jamaicans cooking with pimento wood. Or the smell could be ganja, the Jamaican word for marijuana.

If you see distant smoke coming off fields, that's not the officials burning ganja, it's the farmers burning their sugar cane. Sometimes the ash even falls on the beach.

Don't be offended if someone offers to sell you drugs. These guys are trying to make a living with an illegal trade, but most are polite if you are. Just say "No, thank you."

Tales from the Naked City

And then there was the New Yorker who bragged about smuggling pot from Brooklyn into Jamaica...

Buying and using drugs is illegal in Jamaica. If caught buying or using drugs, you go to Jamaican jail—not a fun prospect.

That said, some guests buy drugs and use them at Hedo. You might be offered drugs anywhere: in the airport, at the bus, or on the beach.

The pharmaceutical boats linger just outside the ropes on the water and come back every half hour or so. That Pssst-Pssst sound you hear is their call for your business. They do not carry Advil. All transactions are negotiable. Where they think naked people keep their wallets is beyond me.

Hedo does not condone the use of drugs or sell it. People who smoke ganja do it in their rooms or at the hot tub. Some smoke it on the edge of the water, on a raft, or after dinner on the far side of the prude pool. If a staff member sees you, you will be asked to put it out. Just take it elsewhere.

The security guards are staff or an agency employed by Hedo for your protection. They aren't with the police.

People who buy more ganja than they use sometimes leave it in the safe in the room for the next guest if they don't pass it to newly arriving guests or friends on the beach. Also check above the closet for a stash.

"Less than five minutes after we got through customs I had a bag of ganja in my hand. I found out later that I got ripped off. Some guys on the bus to Hedo scored some weed from the same dude I scored from. They paid $20 and I paid $40 for the same amount. That's what I get for not haggling over the price. I was really just in a hurry to get some smoke.

As soon as we arrived at Hedo and got checked in, I went directly to the bar for a cold one. Then proceeded to the nearest table to roll a fat one. Damn, this place is the fucking best! The first thing I saw when I lit up the joint was two beautiful, topless women. If I had died right then, I would have died a happy man.

Day 2 my luck got better when it came to buying reefer. I scored well over a half ounce for only $30. I don't remember much about the rest of that day except the wild sights in the nude hot tub.

Day 3: What kind of exciting adventure awaits? Cocaine. I scored a gram for $40. Not only was it cheap, it was 100% pure. This coke was so potent that I had to give half of it away.

These are not the only reasons I went to Jamaica."

—A 22-year-old guy from North Carolina,
April 1996

A friend tells me the cocaine sometimes is cut with lime (I'm not talking fruit) and many people end up in the nurse's station. Although a lot of people smoke ganja at Hedo, no one is guaranteed a good batch.

Jenny's magic tea and brownies are a Negril institution. This roadside restaurant also serves regular food. By eating the entire magic brownie you could miss a day of your vacation. One guy coming back after a visit to Jenny's still had two eyes in his head, but they were each going in an opposite direction.

If you take drugs home with you, the nice doggies at the airport in Jamaica and in the States will smell you out. U.S. drug agents are fierce, and people arriving from Jamaica are their focus.

Some ganja could fall into the cuff of trousers or a pocket and, when you go through customs, you will find out what zero tolerance is all about. Clothes also absorb the smell. One way to avoid that problem is to smoke it on the nude beach away from your bag. If you use a pipe, leave it in Jamaica.

Two brothers came to Hedo—one smoked ganja in the room, the other never touched the stuff. The clean brother was stopped and cavity searched in New York because the smell was in his luggage. He was not happy with his brother.

Sometimes a sting operation is going on: A guy will sell you ganja and momentarily you are arrested. Jamaican jails are less than wholesome.

Tales from the Naked City

There's no way we can top what we did yesterday. *Said by Steve at the breakfast table.*

I can't believe we outdid yesterday. *Said by Steve at the dinner table.*

144

Games you can only play on a nude beach (And we're not talking ring toss)

The guests on the nude beach organize games to entertain themselves. Hedo guests also find ways of improving some hotel games. For example, for body painting, using edible body paints adds a tasty element of fun for the painters. And bringing ribbed mittens to rub the paint off in the beach shower or ocean increases pleasure too.

Tales from the Naked City

It's a fucking yellow line. *Said by Barbara when asked what she was painting on Jim during the body painting contest after doing only one brush stroke.*

Another game specially designed for the nude beach is the guessing game. A friend comes up behind you and puts their hands gently across your face so you can't peek. Then you must feel behind you to guess who it is.

Finding the natural red head is the hardest game to play. This often takes many trips to research. I've found plenty of males, but the female is trickier to find. Then conning her into letting you take of picture of the natural red part so you can prove to the world it exists requires diplomacy.

The nude beach crowd is renown for throwing confetti products. When the Bubbly Bares do it, which is always, the confetti that hits the beach is called Bare Shit. Drunken sources estimate the glitter and paper and metallic confetti make up one-third of the nude beach at Hedo. If you don't bring your own to ornament yourself, you need only roll in the sand to become sparkly.

To torture a friend sleeping on his or her stomach, take a dry straw and blow through it gently along your soon-to-be vengeful buddy's butt crack. The person will awake suddenly in alarm because the air feels like someone dribbling sand into his or her butt.

Another way to stir up trouble, but have a good laugh at someone else's expense, is to walk up to a guy and stuff his penis into a frozen slush drink. The slush sticks to the organ (iced drinks just fall off) making it harder to wipe off, thus maintaining a freezing effect.

If pleasure is more your forte, try the car wash game. Line up two rows of women facing each other, about two feet apart. A man walks the gauntlet between the two lines slowly spinning with his arms about his head and the women have their way as he passes. If you switch the sexes, make sure the men understand about courtesy and respect because some people lose their sanity at the prospect of anonymously touching a passing woman.

Psychic Dick and Breast reading aren't official games, but they too can only be done well on a nude beach. The women all become psychics (a talent no doubt passed down from their wild gypsy grandmothers), and hold a man's future in their hands. For a Vinnie, the standard reading is "Young, dumb, and full of cum." Normally the woman holds onto the penis until tumescence is reached and tells the man, "Things are looking up for you." Men do the breast readings, if they can get away with it.

Another contest that has nothing sexy about it is the pissing contest between men and women. One woman in November with a full bladder beat a man for distance in the grass near the hot tub. And he even had an 8-inch lead.

Hold Up the Towel

Ring toss is not played on the nude beach (even though Hedo has been called the Land of the Organic Sundials) because erections are objects of much joshing to most of the beach crowd. One game does require a hidden erection,

146

though. The game, Hold Up the Towel, requires each male contestant to bring the hand towel from the room to the beach. His team of female experts must inspire him to erection through any means (usually done behind said towel) and once attained, the towel is hung on said erection, and the man can no longer be touched. Female experts may use visual or aural cues to inspire staffs of steel, however.

This is a timed event. The man who can maintain the erection the longest wins. Now, mind you, everyone else is not inspiring the contestant and might even be said to be making the erection falter and waver in its dedication.

Attacking other beaches

About 30 naked people jumped on rafts, armed with water balloons, and floated over the prude beach (Suggestion: Start at the nude beach side of the pier. Most people are drunk and can't paddle too far). As they approached they said nary a word. They just kept getting closer. A guy standing in the water on the prude beach called to them, "You can't come across this line, you're naked." He pointed to the rope. In response they started flinging their powerful weapons, which didn't break, so now the enemy had artillery to return fire. Everyone fell off the rafts and after 10 minutes of bombardment, the leader screamed "Retreat! Run away!" And they paddled away laughing their heads off.

When attacking with balloons, use the light-skin membrane biodegradable balloons. They are usually olive drab green and looked like little hand grenades. Sometimes guards stop guests from using those huge boating slingshots, but you can usually get some good shots in before discovery.

The Sandals manager once called the Hedo general manager to say: "Someone has left your gate open again, and some of your animals have gotten loose. Please come round them up." Likely a brigade of the Butt Crack Tour or a shaving cream swimsuit crowd from the nude beach at Hedo came through at the water line with whistles and huge floats to wave at the sleeping couples of the neighboring hotel. Shaving cream suits look good when you start out, but they tend to drip and melt along the way, which makes them more effective when visiting the front desk to greet newcomers.

Tales from the Naked City

Guests have been staging the choreographed abduction-rape for many years with fun results. We planted our rape victim in swimsuit on the prude beach. (So what if she had improved breasts and no pubic hair?) We promised not to leave her there for more than 10 minutes so she could avoid tan lines. Practice sessions on the nude beach before the raid helped ensure easy swimsuit removal and no suffering to our plant.

Next, about 10 naked middle-aged men ran in single-file military style to the prude beach, calling out "we want women!" The girl sitting next to our plant said: "Oh my god, they're naked. Oh my god, they're running." Our men swarmed around the plant and yee-hawed victoriously as they all picked her up and cast her suit aside and ran with her on their shoulders back to the nude beach. The Prude men desperately sought their cameras, and their women were just glad they weren't picked. (Hint: warn the guards of this event so they don't bust up your game.)

The bidet treatment

Unsuspecting people would see Mr. Cummings, a male sand sculpture on his back carved in the sand, and they were invited to play the game. They first stand over the sand erection. Next they bend over slowly to pluck a plastic eyeball from a cup buried in the man's chest. The garden hose buried

148

beneath the sand under the erection then abruptly shoots forth
and squirts the player.

**Squirting water from a buried hose surprises
Millie from New York.**

Muff Sliding

But the most dangerous sport is Muff Sliding (not to be confused with another sport, Muff Diving) on Delroy's bar.

You can body surf along Delroy's bar—the curved part over the pool. First make the bar counter slick with lots of pool water. Next, lie belly down and wrap arms and legs around the edge of the bar. Push off the concrete pole or have someone shove you off. Hold on for dear life as you make the half-circle curve of the bar. At the end of the curve lies something worth diving for—a girl seated on the bar against a concrete pole with legs spread as a cushion for the incoming sport enthusiast. Safety tip: have friends block the other concrete poles so if centrifugal force sends the contestant off the bar he can live to muff slide again. Reported record time is 1.5 seconds.

Butt Chug

The Butt Chug was developed for men who aren't sure they like beer but want to learn to like it. This performance art requires one reclined male (with or without goggles) and at least one female with a back that arches and has an indent along her spine for the beer to trail down.

The single girl butt chug has the woman straddling the man's face (from a polite height). She can face forward or backward. With arms flung wide to either side for effect and better beer flow, she leans slightly forward and flips her butt up. Then comes the torrents of cold beer (eight glasses should be enough) carefully poured down her back by faithful assistants. As the liquid refreshment slides off her butt, the guy below receives mouthfuls of the amber delight.

The double-girl butt chug aligns the butts of two women, back to back. Ensure that the cracks of the two butts form a tiny diamond shape for the beer to pass through. Again, the women spread arms and teams of beer pourers do their work.

The double-girl cascading butt chug is the highest art on the nude beach and most easily done on the stairs of the cool water Jacuzzi.

The game Butt Chug (especially as a double-girl cascade) helps men who don't like beer learn to love it.

Sink the Raft

Rafting 101 is a class offered at Hedo, but even some vets never passed and consistently slide off the raft at awkward angles. Part of the class requires participants to see how many people can stay on a double raft: 14 is about max before the people at the bottom level drown. One tip: have the people on the bottom lie face up with heads on the pillows. By the third layer of bodies, slip and slide usually takes place.

The $1.99 single raft contest is a greater challenge: seven is the largest number of bodies I know to pile on those flimsy throwaway rafts.

LTN contest

One year Jim had taken about two dozen pictures of ladies' left nipples for what he advertised as his "Left Titty Nipple Contest." He returned the following year with the finished pictures and held the "LTN Contest."

He proudly displayed his creation—a poster full of LTN pictures, each one numbered for the voting. He put the poster in a friend's room window next to the pool so everyone could see and spend all week trying to match the LTN with the ladies present and vote for a favorite. Jim announced the winner poolside a few days later, and Peggy presented the winner, Marilyn, with a brand new jar of udder cream—the same used on milk cows.

Name that dick

This game requires a relatively well-known man to be covered head to toe with the yellow beach towels to annihilate his identity except for his penis, which protrudes between two towels and lies there limply.

The moderator, a man, gathers participants to "name that dick." Everyone tries to figure out who is under the towels.

Participants may pick up the penis and try talking into it and tapping the top, saying, "Hello? Is this thing live? Hello?"

The moderator starts talking about the penis, possibly of its past glory or pitiful future. About a minute into the diatribe, he picks up the penis (actually a woman picks up the penis, but the toweled man thinks the moderator just touched him), and a jolt of horror or surprise is often expressed beneath the towels.

Games for the pools and hot tub

The tables in the pool present new challenges to vertical balance for dancing but are best used as massage tables or venues for photo ops. People gather around the tables and groups can degenerate into parties for bellybutton shots or slippery nipple drinks all applied to appropriate body parts.

Wear glow-in-dark paint at night in the hot tub for a good effect. When women do their breasts, the orbs glow green and look translucent. One man reported the cream chemical was uncomfortable on his penis, so beware.

In the hot tub women can high-four each other. You know the way guys high five each other? Women go it the same way with their breasts and bounce off each other. The timing of the jump dictates whether proper contact is made. Don't do it in the middle of the hot tub, though, you could break a toe if you land wrong on the grate.

Biggest Cup Size

This hot tub game doesn't rely on the massive nature of a woman's breast for winning. When the hard plastic cups at the bar run out, because those darn naked people were drinking heavily again, the bartenders start using soft plastic cups.

Gather these soft cups to use for this game. Using suction, stick one cup on each breast. The best technique usually involves wetting the cup, filling it about one-third to one-half with water, and squeezing in onto the breast to create suction.

Now you have the base for the Biggest Cup Size game. Every cup added to the base cup increases the cup size. One woman had more than seven cups on each breast before the weight made them fall off. Men especially like to help the female contestants grow their cup size.

Muff Diving

This contest of lung capacity is not hard to figure out. What is hard to figure out is why anyone would want to put his face in the hot tub's water. The best time I've recorded (as a judge) was 90 seconds.

The muff diving contest in the hot tub is fun even if your team doesn't win.

The Wave and The Train

Cocktail hour in the hot tub usually instills a giddy attitude into the crowd and in such large groups, collective activities spontaneously occur. The seated conga train of people snaking about the tub is a likely scene. Also, seeing how many people fit in the hot tub is usually at least an annual event around Halloween. The hot tub wave is created when some people all face the same direction in a line and arm in arm and start thrusting their hips in and out together to create a whoosh of water flooding the other side of the hot tub.

Chapter 6

Beyond Hedo

A whole island completely unlike Hedo lies beyond the gates. Check out any travel book for excellent descriptions and suggestions.

Imagine spending an hour listening to two Jamaicans chat. Imagine not understanding a single syllable that comes from their mouths. This is the patois spoken in Jamaica. The best most guests can do is catch single words, such as "policeman," which is what Jamaicans call Red Stripe beer (the Jamaican police often have a red stripe up their pant leg).

Irie. This catch-all greeting means many things—all of them good. As a state of life, irie means "all things are good." As a wish to guests, it means "enjoy your days." Everything is irie. Even better than irie, though, is "Everything is Chris," and even better than that is "Everything is Chris and Curry."

Foo-foo. Should you find yourself near a Vinnie, merely utter the words *foo-foo* to the closest Jamaican and point at the Vinnie casually. *Foo-foo* is someone who is mentally retarded.

Soon come, mon. Island time runs slowly. When a Jamaican says "soon come," that means you must be patient.

The Jamaican people are intensely nationalistic, unlike many of the other smaller Caribbean islands. Their colors are red, green, yellow, and black, and they are worn proudly.

When you return to Hedo and a member of the staff says with a smile that you look like you gained weight, that is a compliment, not an insult.

157

"Once in Jamaica you learn the phrase 'No Problem' and are invited to feel your own personal sense of freedom in every direction in all dimensions...with others doing the same. My newfound freedom was born in the direction of being totally nude with the man I love in front of the world."

—C.K. in California, age 37

Not only do you find yourself picking up the lingo, but you'll likely take home souvenirs. The airport and Hedo charge much the same prices for souvenirs such as coffee, liquor, and jerk spice. Sometimes the airport is less costly. In Negril, though, guests find the best deals.

Rodeo Drive (the nickname for the row of shacks just left and across the road outside of Hedo) offers T-shirts, baskets, and carvings for negotiable amounts. Downtown Negril offers extensive shack shopping.

Cuban cigars, such as Cohiba, cost as little as $8 each in Negril. To reduce the odds of problems when bringing Cuban cigars into the United States (they are illegal to import), remove the cigar band and store them in your bags far from the cigars.

On the nude beach, woodcarvers near the pier sell you naughty and nice carvings of people and fish and the like. But make sure the carving fits in your luggage because crating and shipping via DHL is a multiday effort and might cost $50.

On the prude beach, Rosie and many others expertly put tiny braids in your hair for a negotiable fee (remember to tip). Some guests bring beads to negotiate price. That hair can be on your crotch or your chest hair (remember to cut it out after a handful of days or your skin hurts). No one should be convinced to have his or her whole head done in patchwork. They look stupid.

Eat, drink, sun, and play outside Hedo

Leave Hedo for at least a day or your brain falls out on your shoulder and you'll mistake it for suntan lotion and spread it everywhere. A bus goes to Rick's Café from Hedo almost every late afternoon and returns after sunset.

Early in the week, walk the beach to see what else is between Hedo and Negril. Walking the beach keeps you relatively sober for an afternoon. Take shoes that can get wet because the sand eventually eats away at your feet and there is a stretch where you have to leave the beach. Explore the little restaurants and beer joints along the way.

A concert on the cliffs one night is possible at Sam Sara. Also, or hang out at the Pickled Parrot for water slide or rope swinging into the water. It is the bar where the nude cruise anchors for snorkeling in the caves.

If you'd like to go into town, consider taking one of the taxis outside Hedo. They're less costly than the shuttle offered at the main desk. Negotiate the price before you get in the car. A group can go from Hedo to Rick's or the Pickled Parrot for $10 U.S. each round-trip and spend six hours there.

Try DeBuss for the best jerk chicken. It's five minutes from Hedo on Manley Boulevard (Ho Chi Minh Trail) going toward Negril. An old rusted double-decker tour bus with a tree growing out of it marks the spot. All the cabbies and bus drivers know it. Take out or eat at the jerk shack. They have other food and cold Red Stripe. A large stage and dance floor mark where concerts are held at night. Ziggy Marley showed up one night unannounced. The food is great, but bring a fire extinguisher for your palate.

Cecile's Café offers homemade ice cream. For a nice dinner out, go to Xtabi and walk down the stairs into the caves that greet the ocean.

"For those who enjoy something romantic, try getting up early one day around 6:30 a.m. Take a walk down the beach past Sandals and go as far as you can till you get to the sticky tree...called that because it sticks out into the water and you can't walk around the water side. It's so quiet and peaceful on the beach at that time. No locals, no noisy boats. You will arrive back at the dining room just as they bring out the pastries hot from the ovens."

—Bill from New Jersey, "Hedobill"

If you like massages, look for a great place down the beach half a mile past Sandals. They use aloe from the stalk in a mind-bending massage—at half the cost of Hedo's alternative.

Shed your bathing suit or keep it on at Bloody Bay, a short walk from Hedo, at the far end of Grand Lido. The gorgeous beach there is about 1½ miles of white sand, and the water has no moss or rocks. Walk out 200 feet and the water is chest deep. A restaurant there, with open fire pit, grill rack, a counter top, and a cooler, has cold drinks, and the cook will throw fresh lobster on the fire for you. Enjoy this respite soon, though, new hotels are under construction there in 1998.

Hedo has a rental car agency at the front desk. Or if you are comfortable riding a motorcycle, take a taxi to a bike rental place to rent a Yamaha dirt bike to tour around. Some places even have Harleys. Roads are in especially poor condition with potholes the size of Manhattan everywhere. Watch for people, goats, cows, horses, dogs, and cats, all sleeping on the roads. Many people drive maniacally, and don't forget "left side drive, right side suicide."

To imitate driving in Jamaica but ensure your body parts remain relatively whole, visit the go-cart track across the street from the Poincienta, about a seven-minute walk from Hedo. Tip the attendants a few bucks for some full-contact races.

Other naked or neighboring hotels

No other hotels to date have quite the same ambiance as Hedo. Other places you can be naked, such as Cap d'Agde, France; Club Orient in St. Martin; Eden in Loreto, Baja, Mexico; and Paradise Lakes, Lutz, Fla. These all have their own wonderful flavor, but none is as much silly fun as Hedo no matter how many Hedophiles stay there. A clothing-optional all-inclusive hotel in the Dominican Republic called Orchid Del Sol is a lifestyles resort.

"For those who miss Jamaica and live near Ocean City, Md., try visiting Secrets down on the bay. Walking through the iron gates is like taking a walk into Jamaica. They have all the drinks, including Ting, and serve jerked chicken.

In the summer you can dock your boat there. They provide rafts for the visitors and the staff can serve you on them. The entertainment consists of live reggae bands during the day and evening in the summer months."

—Bill from New Jersey, "Hedobill"

Many hotels in Negril are smaller and less costly, such as Sea Gem (876-957-4318), about a mile from the center of town, near the Kuyaba restaurant. From there, you could check out Hedo for a day or evening to see how you like it.

Hedo sells day and night passes most of the time, but call first. The day pass ($65) buys a day on the beach plus lunch; the night pass ($75) buys dinner and evening entertainment anywhere on campus.

Hedo neighbors: Grand Lido and Sandals

Among themselves, Hedo guests insult guests of the neighboring hotels, Sandals and Grand Lido. Those guests also take great pride is slinging it back at the Zoo guests. Human nature makes us want to have someone close by to poke fun at. That's why people from Illinois call people from Wisconsin Cheeseheads, and Canadians laugh at Newfoundlanders. (But the Newfie handshake is fun—consists of shaking the penis and breast—done between men and women.)

If you want a more sedate pace, try Sandals, an all-inclusive resort for couples next door. Hedo guests say, "If you can't party with the big boys, go to Sandals." Each week the men of Sandals come to challenge the animals at Hedo to a clothed volleyball game. Their wives duly camp out court side, counting the minutes till they can return to the sanctity of Sandals.

Tales from the Naked City

One year the body painting team put one letter of Hedonism II on each cheek of five people. Then all five took a boat to Sandals. As they passed the beach, everyone stuck out their moon in the proper order so it read H E D O N I S M II from the shore. As the boat passed, people on the beach ran away. On the return pass with the same message again showing, the beach had filled with people taking pictures.

—Chris from NW Chicago suburbs

Sandals people seem boring—all paired off on their huge beach with its baby powder soft sand (note the sand envy I bear). Their big excitement seems to be to take a boat cruise of the nude beach with a video camera glued to their eyes.

If you want a more elegant vacation experience, try Grand Lido. Grand Lido, which is also owned by SuperClubs, is also known as Snob Acres and the Grand Dead. Grand Lido lets you shop its ritzy boutiques in the lobby; just show a Hedo room key to the guard. The resort is nice but quiet. People who like to wear jackets or pantyhose for dinner go there. Room service with champagne isn't bad, though.

Each afternoon Grand Lido gives a guided tour of the property. Its 400-year-old humungus cottonwood tree is a must-see. Check at the Hedo front desk for details.

Grand Lido's huge motorized yacht, the Zein, was originally a gift from Aristotle Onassis to Grace Kelly and Prince Rainier of Monaco as a wedding gift. Now SuperClubs owns it. The yacht is available for sunset cruises (reservations with concierge are required). This pleasant cocktail cruise goes past Rick's Café and the Negril Light House on the West End. The cruise includes entertainment and light appetizers—by no means a meal. Its clothing optional cruise is usually on Thursday mornings.

Jo Anne and Bill from New Jersey were the first couple asked to leave the Grand Lido. During the Lido's opening week, the manager walked them from their Lido room to the front gate at Hedo, where the Hedo staff applauded.

A typical day at Grand Lido

By Doug from Pennsylvania

6 a.m. Acknowledge sunrise; call room service to turn off sun.

7 a.m. Call room service to order coffee in room; too humid to go outside.

8 a.m. Room service brings eight-course food to room.

9 a.m. Decide which clothes are politically correct for meals, social activities.

10 a.m. Leave room; hire local to carry belongings to beach.

11 a.m. Have room service bring menu to beach.

Noon Order lunch.

1 p.m. Get slapped for ogling "Fitness Beach" girls.

2 p.m. Realize you left 1,000 SPF sun block in room.

3 p.m. Send room service to get sun block.

3:15 p.m. Think about dinner clothes—suit jacket and tie.

4 p.m. Order cocktails from room service; complain about setting sun.

5 p.m. Six nonalcoholic drinks consumed; sunset no different.

6 p.m. Prepare for dinner, choose clothes, take nap, and apply Solarcaine.

8 p.m. In bed, lights out.

Rinse-lather-repeat.

A typical day at Hedo

By Doug from Pennsylvania

6 a.m. Show map of property to bartender in disco. Ask how to find your room.

6:01 a.m. Bartender turns map right-side up—problem solved.

9 a.m. Room found.

164

Noon Potty break—check pulse.

1 p.m. Realize, as a man, you look good in a crotchless G-string.

2 p.m. Sit on edge of bed. Realize you are spontaneously breathing with no assistance.

3 p.m. Stand.

3:01 p.m. Floor looks neat; note dust bunnies under bed.

3:30 p.m. Breakfast: A glass of water from the bathroom.

4:15 p.m. Locate first bar. Use sign language to order first drink. Have a piña colada—just like in the brochure.

4:16 p.m. Lean on bar.

4:30 p.m. Get smacked for telling guy he has "a cute butt."

5 p.m. Pitcher of Hummingbirds ordered. Head to hot tub.

5:10 p.m. Return to bar for pitcher of Hummingbirds.

6 p.m. Re-arrive at hot tub. Pitcher is empty. New friends found en route.

7 p.m. Comment on great underwater action.

7:22 p.m. Realize your hand is providing the action.

8 p.m. Crawl to room to prepare for dinner.

1 a.m. Wake for dinner.

1:05 a.m. Run to dining area for last call for food.

1:10 a.m. Return to room for clothes.

1:30 a.m. Go to disco to watch people.

6 a.m. Repeat.

Your mileage may vary. Couples, committed singles, and persons of unknown or unspecified sexual orientation need not apply. This offer not valid in Montego Bay, Lucea, Kingston, or Ocho Rios. See your dealer for details.

Hedonism III going up near Runaway Bay

SuperClubs has broken ground for Hedonism III on a 10-acre site 40 minutes from MoBay in Runaway Bay (toward Ocho Rios). Scheduled for completion before 2000, the hotel will consist of 220 rooms, four restaurants, three swimming

pools, land sports, extensive entertainment facilities including a disco, and a nude pool and beach facilities. Its heavily land-scaped gardens feature many water focuses such as waterfalls, water slides, misting pools, and hot tubs.

The new Hedo will have all the same activities, such as toga night, as the old one with slightly fewer people and less spread in hotel land. Hedo II general manager Kevin Levee says he doesn't know what the differences in ambiance will be because everything about Hedo is guest generated; he expects it to evolve. He'll be contacting old-timers (in coming years) to talk about trying the new Hedo.

Guests traditionally use Hedo's Moon Hill to say good-bye to a busload of friends.

Use the Internet for year-round Hedo

Many Internet sites talk about and show photos of Hedo, nudism, lifestyles, and Jamaica. All addresses start: http://

www.super-clubs.com/Hedonism.html

Travel agents:
www.playcouples-travel.com/hedo.html
(Lifestyles Tour and Travel)
www.gonude.com (Go Classy Tours)

Some Hedophiles have their own sites about Hedo:
members.aol.com/hedolistic/ (tons of Hedo links)
www.dennyp.com (msg. board, guest list, trip reports)
ourworld.compuserve.com/homepages/JAMAICAJIM/
members.aol.com/flashem1/Hedo2.html
members.aol.com/contraband/
home.sprynet.com/sprynet/dgande/
www.biffsbunch.com/
members.aol.com/hedophile/index.htm
www.angelfire.com/ms/upallhedo/ (Frank & Marcey)

Sites offering nudism info:
www.paradiselakes.com (nudist community near Tampa)
www.sunnyrest.com (nudist park in Poconos)
www.naturist.com (The Naturist Society)
www.aanr.com (American Assoc. for Nude Recreation)
www.tanr.com (Tanning and Nude Recreation)

For news and info about Jamaica or Negril:
www.jamaica-gleaner.com
www.beingees.com/beingee2.htm
jamaicaconnection.com
USA Today weather report for MoBay:
www.usatoday.com/weather/basemaps/nw783880.htm

AOL Hedo message board

To find current poop on Hedo, look at the Hedonism II message board on AOL. In AOL, click Travel on the Channel dialog box, and then choose Messages & Chat. Next choose Travel Destination Message Boards, Caribbean, All-Inclusive, and Hedonism II. The message board only lists responses you haven't read yet unless you click List All before getting there.

Typical entry on AOL Hedonism II message board:

"Gator woman,

How could anyone forget that smile? It lights up the beach in broad daylight. Your boobs aren't bad either. I have to hold Eric back with a chair. He has orchestrated this like Quido the guide. Don't worry we will not start without you and Dr. Chris. It wouldn't be a party without you guys. Bye the bye, I am placing the order for the Alien masks this week. I've been practicing sex and booze every night."

The End
Till the next trip.

Author biography

Chris Santilli is a freelance writer living in Villa Park, Ill.
Her first book, *Career Opportunities in Masonry*, was pub-
lished in 1993. She lives with her fat black cat, Joe.

Glossary

Delroy's

Nude beach bar near the property line of Hedo and Point Village, named for its bartender whiz, Delroy Roache. The old Delroy's bar is in the center of the nude beach.

Fornicatorium

The area behind the waterfall in the nude pool complex that can seat six to eight comfortably. Parties of more than 40 are possible. Also known as BJ Cave or BJ Grotto.

Ganja

Marijuana

MoBay

The Jamaican nickname for Montego Bay. They call Ocho Rios *Ochi*.

Nude

A person who spends most of his or her day naked on the nude beach.

Pastafari

Air-conditioned Italian sit-down restaurant next to main dining area. Open for dinner 6 p.m. to 1 a.m. Requires reservations unless the night is slow and room is available. Guests order from a twice-weekly changing menu, and a wait staff serves. Champagne is available in Pastafari. Daily access included in resort package. Shoes are required.

Prude

A person who spends most of his or her day clothed in a swimsuit on the prude beach or at the prude pool.

Repeater

Any guest who is at Hedo at least a second time. Also called repeat-offender. Some guests have been to Hedo more than 50 times.

Sea urchin

Small spiny sea creature that releases its spines when stepped on. Causes extreme pain. Island cure is to pee on the affected area (the ammonia dissolves the spines). Most people go to the nurse.

Veronica's

The piano bar near the dining area is named for its premier bartender, who is always quick with a smile and your beverage of choice. Also look for bartender Sujean there. (Delete has moved to the tour desk.) This bar has the best call brands but no blender drinks. It has a game room and gambling machines on either side of the bar.

Vinnie

An under 35, usually male, person who doesn't exhibit courtesy.

Wally

A single male, Nude or Prude, who stares a great deal and doesn't say much, usually older than 35.

Index

Lunchtime spin 126, 127

M

Marian from Pennsylvania 20
Marilyn's T-shirt 110
Marina and George 51
Marley, Ziggy, 159
Marriage (see Wedding)
Master Spike and Slave Joey 116
Masturbation 10
Matt the Mayor 42, 96
Mayonnaise party 108
McLean, George, 66
Meal times 40
Media at Hedo 57
Medical concerns (see health)
Meeting people 16
Mike's reef 132
Millie from New York 19, 149
Mirrors 30
Miss Hedonism contest 136
Misting pool 71
Money 18
Moon Hill 166
Mosquitoes 54
Motor cycles 160
Mud Slide 44
Muff Diving 154
Muff Sliding 150

N

Name that Dick game 152
Natural fashion show 123, 126, 127
Negril 158
Negril Beach Club Village 21
Negril Stinger 45
Newfie handshake 162
Nicknames 94
Night Calls, Playboy, 57
Night dives 133

Night pass ($75) 161
No Problem, a drink, 45
Non Smoking 34
Nudes 59, 69
Nudity 8, 46, 65, 138
Nurse 54

O

Older than dirt 94
Oliver from West Chester, Pa. 127
On the Edge 91

P

Packing 16, 17, 49
Panties, 1, 17, 79, 139
Parfumier 46, 79, 86
Passes to Hedo 161
Pastafari 39, 40
Pasternak, Denny, 59, 69, 134
Paul from New York 97
Pelican 74
Photography 22, 47
Piano bar 137
Pickled Parrot 135, 159
Pickup lines 114
Piercing (see Body art)
Pimento wood 142
Pinpals 90
Pissing contest 146
Playboy 57
Point Village 27, 79
Pool, nude, 70
Poopsie 90
Poverty 22
Power outages 28
Prizes 124
Prudes 59, 69
Psychic dick and breast readings 146
Purple Rain 44

Quick Reference Numbers

Hedonism II
P.O. Box 25, Negril P.O., Jamaica, West Indies
General Manager: Kevin Levee
876-957-5200 (main phone) also: 876-957-5204 to 08
876-957-5289 (accounting fax)
876-957-5055 (general manager's fax)
876-957-5214 (general fax)

Air Jamaica
800-523-5585 (flight info and reservations)

SuperClubs
P.O. Box 222800, Hollywood, FL 33022
800-859-7873 or 800-GO-SUPER (800-467-8737)

TimAir
MoBay: 876-952-2516; fax: 876-987-1113
also: 876-979-1114 or 876-940-7766 or 876-979-5369
Negril: 876-957-5374

Air Negril
Reservations: 876-940-7746
Head office: 876-940-7751
fax: 876-940-6491

Aero Express
MoBay: 876-952-5807
Negril: 876-957-9113

Color Negril, Ltd.
Robin Farquharson, President
Coral Seas Plaza, P.O. Box 63, Negril, Jamaica, W.I.
876-957-4594; fax: 876-957-4595

Want Another Book?
Order One!

Your friends will giggle about the high jinks that go on at Hedonism II. Why not order a copy as a gift?

Call toll-free 888-883-9040

(Monday through Friday, 8:30 a.m. to 5 p.m. central time)
Visa and MasterCard accepted.

To order one to four books, send $19.95 per book, plus $3.45 each for shipping & handling (total each: $23.40).

Illinois residents, please add $1.35 per book (for 6.75% sales tax), making the total $24.75.

Please make your check or money order in U.S. dollars payable to **Scarlett, Oh! Publishing**

Send name, address, payment, and quantity desired to:

P.O. Box 6584 ● Villa Park IL 60181-6584

Orders ship first-class within one week of order receipt. Discounts are available for five or more books; for more information write the above address, call toll-free at 888-883-9040, or e-mail Books@wordcrafting.com.

www.wordcrafting.com/hedobook.stm

Thanks for your interest!